I want to dedicat
to Dwane and Ant
God helped me
parents. I will see

Love
Aldo

TO

My heavenly Father for His love and grace in my life;

Jesus for His precious blood;

The Holy Spirit, my best Friend, for picking me up.

TO

Tinus for your determination and for being patient with Aldo. Thank you for everything you do to help me. Know that I see each little thing and I appreciate it. We've been leaning on you a lot and I'm grateful, now more than ever, that your Foundation is strong. Thanks again!

Josh, you are the smile in our lives; the sunshine amidst the rain. I love you dearly!

Aldo, my champ!

 Please note that Destiny Image's publishing style capitalizes certain pronouns in Scripture that refer to the Father, Son, and Holy Spirit, and may differ from some publishers' styles. Take note that the name satan and related names are not capitalized. We choose not to acknowledge him, even to the point of violating grammatical rules.

Consulting Publisher: Corals Publishers
Translator and editor: Henriette Visser
Cover design and Layout: Tanya Lonbard

DESTINY IMAGE® PUBLISHERS, INC.
P.O. Box 310, Shippensburg, PA 17257-0310
"Speaking to the Purposes of God for this Generation and for the Generations to Come."

This book and all other Destiny Image, Revival Press, Mercy Place, Fresh Bread, Destiny Image Fiction, and Treasure House books are available at Christian book-stores and distributors worldwide.

For a U.S. bookstore nearest you, call 1-800-722-6774.
For more information on foreign distributors, call 717-532-3040.
Or reach us on the Internet: www.destinyimage.com

ISBN 13: 978-0-7684-6432-0

Previously published as ISBN 13: 978-0-7684-3051-6

Previously published as ISBN 978-0-620-38441-4 by Retha Mc Pherson

For Worldwide Distribution, Printed in the U.S.A.

1 2 3 4 5 6 7 8 9 10 11 / 13 12 11 10 09

a message from god

Preface

I've always confessed that I'm a Christian. I've always known God. I believed in the Holy Trinity and I even served God.

Yet, when I look back now I realize that I was merely living a good life filled with good deeds. I didn't really know God's character and I had no idea what it meant to be completely sold out to Him – which is the only sacrifice that is ever acceptable in His sight! I had to live through a terrible tragedy and huge suffering, before I was finally willing to sacrifice everything, including my son, to God. Only after all that, did I hand over control of my life to Him and did I get to know Him personally. All this pain was so unnecessary! Jesus had already paid the price in full. After I had given my life to Him as a living sacrifice, I could get in line with God's perfect plan for my life, i.e. to live in a love relationship with the living God. Only then could I say that it didn't matter whether I lived or died, as long as I glorified God.

The first part of this book tells the story of how a picture-perfect family became an utterly broken one, desperately clinging to God and His promises. In the second section you will find both the messages (insights) that the Holy Spirit has imparted to my son

Aldo, as well as my own reflections on these issues. God, who works in mysterious ways, has done so again, speaking simultaneously to both Aldo and I about the same issues. I believe that what we've written is in line with Scripture and I invite you to test our thoughts to the Word of God.

Our main purpose with this book is to tell people that Jesus lives! He is a great and awesome God who wants your life, not only your heart, and He is coming back for a spotless bride: those who will lay down their lives as a living sacrifice to Him. Aldo and I want you to know that God still performs miracles in our day and age and that He wants to fill you with His Holy Spirit and have a love relationship with you.

You are not holding a mere book in your hands today. You are looking at a message straight from the Father's heart to everyone who reads it. Let he who has an ear, listen to what the Spirit is saying.

I pray that the Spirit of God within you will awaken and that you'll feel it burning inside of you as you read this book. If you are looking for God, I know you will find Him, for He promises, "those who look for Me, shall find Me".

For a long time I thought it was my husband's responsibility to make me happy, but the truth is no human being can make you completely happy. Only Jesus can do that for you. He is the ANSWER to all questions; the SOLUTION to all problems; the FULFILMENT of all your needs and desires. He is ALL things to ALL men! I tried to quench my thirst with all sorts of things like perfectionism, fame, wealth and achievement. But, now that the fire of the Holy Spirit has purified me from the inside out, I know Jesus is the fountain of living water. He is the only One who can quench my thirst forever.

Jesus wants to baptise us with the Holy Spirit.

1 Cor. 3:13 teaches us that the works of each person will be tested by fire and the fire will reveal the character and worth of the work each one has done. When you are baptised in the Holy Spirit, and receive its fire, you'll experience the fullness of God. Only then can you become a light to the dark world.

God works in the lives of people so that they may become pure of heart and fully comitted to Him.

Nowadays I just can't get enough of God. I want to spend every possible minute in prayer, praising and honoring Him. One must be reborn of the Spirit, because only once you've been filled by the Spirit, will you be able to live a life of abundance that Jesus talks about in Jn. 10:10.

This life of abundance has little to do with your bank balance, or material wealth. Simply put it means living a life utterly saturated with God. I believe that the principles I have penned down in the second part of the book not only elaborates on what Aldo has written, but also serve as guidelines for every believer who desires a closer walk with our Lord Jesus.

Know one thing for sure: Jesus is alive!

PART 1
OUR STORY

LIVING THE DREAM

It was the year 2004 and perhaps the best year of my life. Things were truly going smoothly and I was successful in everything I started.

I had lived my entire life trying to serve God, and had always put my heart and soul into everything I did, thinking it to be synonymous with being a Christian. Thus, I suppose I had put my success down to the fact that I had always given my best in everything I did. But God would show me the folly of this type of thinking. While sitting on the beach one day, God spoke to me and said, "Retha, the Lion of Judah lives within you". Being still so much of this world, I thought that God was telling me that there was yet more for me, and that I had to work harder to attain it. I would have to set the bar even higher and do even better, because He had, after all, given me the ability to do so. But this was only a half-truth: Yes, the Lion of Judah does live in us and, yes God wants to give us the absolute best of everything, but we cannot attain it through our best efforts. It is a free gift from God. To me, at that stage in my life, God's "best" meant the quantity and quality of material possessions that I could gather – material wealth! I've always rationalized that the harder I worked, the more I would have and the greater would be the testimony of God's goodness and favor in my life!

I was a churchgoer and member of a renewal congregation. We were religious, but we were spiritually dead. There was a void in me and I didn't know how to fill it. I was desperate to find whatever was missing from my life. I did everything I could think of to fill the emptiness inside: Bible studies, retreats, women's camps, but nothing brought me to the place where I could make a complete commitment. It seemed that a spiritually fulfilled and abundant life was always out of my grasp. *"Life in the full,"* that Jh. 10:10 refers to was not a reality for me.

All my hard work bore fruit. Early in 2004, I was privileged to attend both a seminar and congress in Canada and New York respectively as an image consultant. I remember sitting on a park bench in Canada one day, while it was snowing. I saw a tree, having lost all its leaves, reaching its stark, naked arms heavenward. The scene was wrapped in brilliant white and complete silence enveloped me. Then the

Spirit of God spoke clearly to me.

He said, "Retha, I want your life."

In ignorant arrogance my spirit answered, "Lord, my heart has been yours for years now. What do you mean?"

"I don't want your heart. You've given it to many men before. I want your entire life; your being; your very essence."

I was taken aback and could only stare out ahead of me. I've tried so many times before to live a better life, I thought. The only reply I could think of was, "Lord, I would love to give You my life, but I just don't know how to do it."

My husband, Tinus, and my eldest son, Aldo, who was 12-years-old at the time, joined me in New York. We went sightseeing and visited the United Nations building. There I was struck by a huge mosaic which depicted all the nations, peoples and languages of the world. My spirit was moved the instant that I saw it. The Spirit said, "All the broken pieces of your life are nothing more than the beautiful mosaic of your future." I knelt and wrote it down on the admission slip. Then I took a picture of this image that would have such relevance to my life in days to come, with Aldo standing beside it.

Aldo was your typical teenager at that time. TOYS "R" US was his favorite New York haunt and at home he played cricket and soccer when he wasn't gallivanting on the quad bike. He was just an everyday teenager. Did he serve God? Well, he attended a youth church regularly and had been on a youth camp right before the accident had happened. In fact, when he'd returned from the camp, he confirmed that he had accepted Christ as his personal Savior. Whenever I would ask him about the services at his youth church, he would always give me the thumbs up and with a lollipop tucked in his jaw, he'd say, "It was great!"

After Aldo was born, we prayed for years to have another child. When Aldo was four-years-old, God gave us a prophetic promise through a black man, Louis Maphungu, that we would have another baby and that it would be a boy. We had to wait some six years more before Josh arrived. Eventually, there would be a ten-year gap between my boys, but I know that God's timing is always perfect, even if we don't feel that way most of the time. Josh was only two-and-a-half-years-old at the time of our 2004 US trip.

I was crowned Mrs. South Africa later in 2004. It opened many doors for me and it was very good for my business. Even then, I knew in my heart of hearts that there was a reason why I got the title. Upon our return from New York, I had to deliver an address at the State Theatre in my official capacity as Mrs. South Africa. I realized that I'd been given a platform and put much thought into the topic of my speech. I asked God what I should talk about and He reminded me of the message He'd given me in New York.

So, I shared my simile of our lives as clay tablets; works of art that we're improving upon daily. We each paint our own tablet. While some of our tablets are bright and beautiful, full of color and life, others are drab, with only beige and brown paint signifying an unfulfilled life. More important though, is what happens once your precious clay tablet slips from your fingers one day and falls to pieces at your feet. No matter the color of your tablet, once it's shattered you will bow your knee to inspect the damage. Bowing down to the broken pieces of your life is an automatic reaction. One person bows down and picks up the pieces. Then, under the guidance of the Holy Spirit, he redesigns his picture, pasting the potsherds to create a new mosaic. Because, "all the broken pieces of your life are nothing more than the beautiful mosaic of your future". Another person kneels down among his destruction. He too collects the pieces, but then he sits in it – defeated. It cuts him and he bleeds. Every time you pass by, you see him still sitting there among the fragments of his life, bleeding. He cherishes his pain and bitterness flows from it.

Today I know, although I didn't realize it at the time, that life is all about choices.

> GOD CREATED US WITH A FREE WILL SO THAT WE CAN CHOOSE. YOU CAN CHOOSE TO RE-SCULPT A NEW PICTURE FROM YOUR FRAGMENTS, WAITING ON THE HOLY SPIRIT TO GUIDE YOU, OR YOU CAN CHOOSE SELF-PITY AND BECOME EMBITTERED.

As I was speaking that night, I could see that the audience was moved by the message. On my way home, I marvelled that I actually had no idea what I was talking about. My life was so perfect. I had a wonderful loving marriage, two beautiful, healthy children, and a successful business. I had just moved into my dream house, was driving a brand-new four-wheel drive vehicle and was named Mrs. South Africa! What a beautiful, color-rich tablet!

Still living the dream, I continued to speak around the country. After just such an engagement I returned home from Port-Elizabeth and Tinus picked me up from the airport. We proceeded directly to Zonderwater

Correctional Facility (near Pretoria) where I would also deliver an address. I didn't really prepare a specific talk for Zonderwater and thus I was quite annoyed with Tinus when he asked me what my speech for that night was about. I simply said, "You know what the people in prison are like". Little did I know that God had a very specific appointment with me that night.

It turned out to be a red-carpet event, with several ministers attending the function. One of the prisoners testified right before I was to speak. He used to be a businessman and had committed white-collar crime. It was heart-wrenching to hear how his family was suffering because of it, with his children having to tell others at school that their father was overseas. "Still, the man you see here tonight is a much happier man. It's the happiest I've ever been," he testified. Then he thanked God for letting him go to prison, "... because this is where I found God. This is where I met and came to know the King of kings". I remember thinking of 1 Thes. 5:18: *"Give thanks in all circumstances, for this is God's will for you in Christ Jesus."* He elaborated that the scales had fallen from his eyes and he had come to know the Truth. He'd asked Christ into his life and was truly set free.

At that stage, tears were streaming down my face. I guess the joke was on me, because I clearly had no idea what the people in prison are really like. Tinus wanted to know why I was so upset.

"That man has something we don't have" I said.

"What? An orange jump suit?" asked Tinus, trying to cheer me up.

The speaker had the peace of God that transcends all understanding and that's what I wanted, although I couldn't put my finger on it back then. I told Tinus that I could see the glory of God on this man and I desired *that* more than anything.

When I got up to speak, I asked the audience if they too were struck by this man's testimony, but sadly only a few hands went up. I guess they were skeptical that God could change a man like that…

I cried all the way home. My tears literally spattered against the car's window. Tinus was quiet, not knowing what to say. When we got home, I knelt and prayed earnestly. "Son of David, have mercy on me. Help me, Lord. I want what that man in prison has." In the calm that followed, He answered, "Retha, my Son came for everyone. But there is a price to what *you* want".

"What is that price, Lord? I'll pay it right now."

"You have to lay down your life. I want your life."

Suddenly I remembered the park bench in Canada and sitting in the snow. God had asked for my life then too.

I REALIZED THAT I HAD ALWAYS TRIED TO EARN MY SALVATION. NOW JESUS WAS SAYING HE DIDN'T WANT THAT. I HAD TO HAND OVER CONTROL OF MY LIFE.

"All right, Lord," I said, "You can have my life. Just show me how to do it."

It is ironic that I, as Mrs. South Africa, had so many opportunities to testify, and yet I didn't know how to do it. Something was always missing.

POTSHERDS

The very next Saturday, I had to speak in the Free State and because we always tried to include the whole family in these activities, we all traveled there together. On our way back, we stopped at a service station and Aldo bought just about all the sweets and candy in the store. Although I usually don't allow this, I let him be that night. As we pulled away, Aldo was handing out sweets, talking excitedly about the new candy that was available. He was so animated, so busy with his narration, that he didn't fasten his seat belt. Neither did Josh.

We'd only gone a short distance from the service station, when my precious tablet fell from my hands and shattered into a million pieces.

Traveling down a hill, we suddenly came upon a stationary vehicle. It had no lights and there were no hazards to warn us. It appeared as if out of nowhere. We all shouted, "Watch out!" but it was too late. Tinus couldn't swerve to the right as we would've been hit by the fast-moving oncoming traffic. He also couldn't go straight as we'd have plowed through the vehicle ahead, almost certainly killing both them and us. The only option was a deep watercourse to our left.

The impact was bone crushing. The instant we hit the watercourse, our vehicle overturned. The car flipped over several times more. I lost consciousness and when I regained it, I immediately struggled out of the car. I stumbled over the wreckage and fell down in the tar road. Again I heard God's voice saying, "All the broken pieces of your life are nothing more than the beautiful mosaic of your future". In that moment, I knew exactly what I was talking about less than a week ago.

"Oh God, no! Not this. Not this!" my spirit screamed.

I found Tinus, but I couldn't locate the children. We started searching frantically for them in the dark, anxiously calling out their names. Not only my voice, but my entire being was calling out for my children. Despite the noise from speeding cars on the highway, I heard the faintest moaning sound. I suppose it was because all my senses, my entire being, were so completely tuned in to my children.

If only I'd been as tuned in to God when He spoke to me in Canada! The first lesson God taught me that night was that my being was not focused on Him.

Although God was speaking to me, I wasn't tuned in to Him and so I couldn't really hear what the Spirit was saying to me. Rev. 3:13 is so important to each Christian. It reads: *"He who has an ear, let him hear what the Spirit says to the churches."*

We heard Josh crying. Relief and fear competed for dominance in my heart. Thankfully he'd only suffered a few cuts to his head. Everyone who arrived at the scene, started searching for Aldo, but none of us could find him. I started screaming his name again, all the while praying for the blood of Jesus to cover my children. "The blood of Jesus, the blood of Jesus," I repeated.

The Spirit of God led me to the other side of the highway. Even now it is painful to recall it. "He won't be over there, Retha. It's too far away," Tinus shouted to me. Just then, I stumbled and fell over Aldo's body. My hands fluttered over his broken body and I touched his head. His scull was cracked and hot blood was trickling from his ears. I felt for a pulse, and when I couldn't find one, I ripped open his bulky snow jacket that we had bought in Canada. I pressed my ear to his chest hoping to hear a heartbeat. There was none.

> IT REALLY DOESN'T MATTER WHO YOU ARE, OR HOW MUCH MONEY YOU HAVE. GOD ALONE HAS POWER OVER LIFE AND DEATH.

I felt my child's life slipping from my fingers and I was completely powerless to stop it.

He is the One who gives life, but He also takes it. I was scared to death that my son would die.

A vehicle was making its way towards us and I instinctively knew I had to stand up and get their attention. The headlights were sharp, piercing the night and shone directly in my eyes. I realized that my whole body was strangely shaking; convulsing. Then a warmth enveloped me and a supernatural peace that I couldn't explain filled me, amidst all the fear, pain and anxiety.

I called over to Tinus and showed them where I had found Aldo. The emergency personnel rushed over and attended to him. A rescue helicopter was summoned. The paramedics made a hole in his lungs, because they had collapsed. They bandaged his head. They assured us that they were qualified and competent, but added that Aldo was badly injured.

But would he live?

They couldn't say.

FRUITS OF THE TONGUE

Many cars had stopped, either out of curiosity or to offer help. One car in particular bore down on us and only stopped a few meters from us. A black man got out quickly. I was frightened, wondering what he was up to. But then he started shouting at the top of his voice, "In the mighty name of Jesus Christ, this boy will live! He will not die. This boy will live and he will not die!" He just kept on shouting this affirmation. The paramedics tried to push him aside because of the noise he was making, but he wouldn't stop. I was confused by this and my spirit called, "Where are you, Lord?" His answer? "Look at that man. Right now, he is my hands and my feet."

We found out later that this man, who was the first to pronounce life over my son, was in fact a pastor from Nigeria who had taken the wrong off-ramp when he came upon the accident. We are still in contact with him today and I can only marvel that God truly does work in mysterious ways.

Today I know that God was there with us. God was in our midst. I felt like Moses who, when realizing his human weakness asked, "Where are You?" God's answer in Exodus is that He is with us during the most difficult times of our lives.

The helicopter landed and Aldo was transported to a hospital in Johannesburg. The emergency operation lasted four hours. When the doctor finally emerged, the news wasn't good. He told us that Aldo had sustained multiple brain injuries. His brain stem, the mid-, left and central parts of the brain were all damaged. He couldn't promise us that Aldo would live, much less make any determination about him making a full recovery.

They put Aldo on life support in the Intensive Care Unit (ICU). We knew the odds that Aldo would be anything other than severely handicapped, were small. His very life was hanging in the balance. Chances that his organs would start failing were high. My child was laying in a glass room in ICU! His head was terribly swollen and monitors were attached to it to monitor the intra cerebral bleeding, which was steadily increasing. As the hemorrhaging increased, the alarms on the monitors would go off. It was nerve-racking. We watched from behind the glass, never taking our eyes off those monitors and graphs.

It was the worst day of our lives, and yet I was calm. Tinus and I didn't speak much. We were struggling with our thoughts of self-blame and guilt. Nothing I said consoled Tinus. He and Aldo had always been very close and he felt responsible for the accident. Utterly devastated, he kept on saying that it was his fault. I denied it and told him that he didn't put the stationary vehicle in the road; that he had no way of knowing it would be there; that he'd done the best he could under the circumstances. But it was no use. Tinus blamed himself because he was Aldo's dad and he had been driving. The enemy, who goes around like a roaring lion (1 Pet. 5:8) had convinced Tinus that he was guilty, and Tinus believed the lie.

But I was blaming myself too. Satan tried to tell me that we weren't worthy of having children. Look what had happened to our children, because of me, I thought. If only I'd gone to that speaking engagement by myself, the children would have been safe at home. If only I were stricter about wearing safety belts. And so, both Tinus and I struggled through the longest night of our lives. Later, I went to sit with Josh who'd been admitted for observation, while Tinus stayed with Aldo.

Was the accident God's will? No, but I believe He allowed it to happen. I know from Scripture that not a single hair will fall from my head, without God knowing about it. So God must have known about the accident, before it even happened, but He allowed it to accomplish His purposes.

> I REALIZED THAT IF I WASN'T CAREFUL THE ACCIDENT COULD DOMINATE MY LIFE, AND THEN I WOULDN'T BE ABLE TO SERVE GOD ANYMORE.

I found comfort in 2 Chr. 16:9, *"For the eyes of the Lord range throughout the earth to strengthen those whose hearts are fully committed to him"*. That's why I know that God was, and still is, with us in our suffering.

We spent the next week going from one doctor to another, looking for some scrap of hope that we could hold on to. The doctors did what they could: They inserted a tube into Aldo's stomach and put a trachea in his throat. He'd broken his collarbone and a few ribs too. His eyes were static and swollen shut. It's ironic, but he didn't have a single bruise on his face.

We were inundated with letters, e-mails and messages of support from people all over the country. The outpouring of love and support was tremendous and I was stunned by it. There was even a letter from Nelson Mandela in which he encouraged us to stay strong. I realize now that the people of South Africa, people who really cared, carried us through this ordeal.

After spending a week in a room across from ICU, Tinus suggested I go home for a bit to spend some time with Josh, who had hardly seen me in that time and who also needed me. But when I left the hospital that Friday night, I was afraid to go home; afraid that Aldo would die. Job 3:25 warns us that whatever you fear, will happen to you. I know from personal experience that it's true. I have always feared that my family and I would be involved in a car wreck and that my children would be hurt. Many times I spoke it out loud too. If Tinus were driving just a little too fast when we were traveling, I would warn him that if something were to happen to us, he would be responsible. Now my words had come back to haunt me... and Tinus.

By fearing and speaking that fear, I had unwittingly given the devil an open door to attack us. God says in

2 Cor. 10:5 that we have to capture every thought and make it obedient to Christ. I have since had to confess and bind all these fears and thoughts in the name of Jesus.

I went home with my heart filled with fear. On Saturday night I was rocking Josh in my arms and was pleased to see that, except for a small cut to his head, my youngest had come through the ordeal largely unhurt. He recounted the accident in great detail; emphasizing that the car had flipped over and over. Then he said that Jesus had caught him when he was flying through the air. At his age, could he really have made it up?

After Josh had fallen asleep, my tears came. For the first time since the accident, I cried. And once I started crying, I couldn't stop. Later I thought my head would explode with pain and I wondered how Aldo had to be suffering from his head injury. I stumbled through the quiet house, weeping. Aldo's room was neat; complete with his soccer ball on his bed and in the kitchen his suitcase was exactly where he'd put it the previous Friday after school. I couldn't stand the silence in the house and I wept and wept.

I finally fell asleep, only to have the most vivid dream. I dreamt I was standing next to Aldo who was lying on his hospital bed. His fingers became black and started shrivelling. What I had feared was happening. In my dream I speak to Aldo and tell him that I can see he is dying. I tell him that I'm letting him go so that he can go to Jesus, since I know that he had accepted Christ on that youth camp. Then Aldo answers me, saying, "Mommy don't say it. Speak life over me. Speak life."

I remembered how we would say goodbye every morning when he went to school. With his backpack over his shoulder, I'd ask him what the password was, and he'd say, "Surely goodness and mercy shall follow me all the days of my life. Love you." We would repeat this ritual when he came home again in the afternoon. "Surely goodness and mercy shall follow me all the days of my life. Love you." So it really wasn't all that strange for Aldo to ask me to pronounce life over him. We'd always done it.

In my dream I then said, "You *will* live, and you'll have life to the full." I kept on repeating it until it became a refrain.

John 10:10 came to me then: *"The thief comes only to steal and kill and destroy; I have come that they may have life, and have it to the full."*

I didn't realize it at the time, but I wasn't merely uttering words, I was speaking life to his spirit. After a while I could see color returning to his lips and his fingers stretching out again. Then he started crying. His crying woke me up on Sunday morning although I was at home, and my child was in hospital, far away. It was also the last time I ever heard him cry. It's been three years since the accident, and till this day, I haven't heard him cry once. He just makes a funny little sound sometimes, and I know that is how he cries.

Waking up from Aldo's crying, I sat up bewildered. I didn't know what was happening to me. I didn't know that God still spoke to His children in dreams today. And yet, He does. He speaks to us through His Word, through dreams, visions, nature and people. In fact, God is continuously speaking to us; we are just not always listening; we're not tuned in to Him, and cannot hear the soft voice of the Holy Spirit whispering to us. In Is. 59:1, God says that His arms are not too short to save us, nor are His ears deaf to hear our pleas. The presence of sin in our lives is like a wall between God and us, keeping us from hearing His voice. When people say they feel like their prayers are bouncing off the ceiling, I know it is impossible. It's not the ceiling that keeps you from making contact with God. It's sin; those things that seem insignificant in our eyes, like jealousy, bitterness, your own strong will, and pride. God hates pride.

After my dream, I couldn't wait for daybreak. I got Josh ready very early and we went to the hospital directly. There I found Tinus in the hallway. He was overcome by sadness and was crying profusely. I asked him what the matter was and he said, "We very nearly lost Aldo around two o'clock this morning". I told him that I knew about it and had seen it play out in my dream. I could see that Tinus was shocked and that he didn't believe me. I don't mean to discredit my husband when I say this, but both he and I were still spiritually dead and until that point we'd never had such experiences in the Holy Spirit. Before the accident we were blind, but now we see. We were dead before, but today we live! I thank God that even through this tragedy He's touched both our spirits and awoken us to Him. I guess He was already rebuilding the beautiful mosaic of our future.

I told Tinus all about my dream and how Aldo had asked me to pronounce life over him. I told him how his shrivelled, black fingers started growing again and how his lips regained their color as I declared that he would live and have life in abundance. Tinus agreed that we would only speak life from then on.

God tells us in Prov. 18:21: *"The tongue has the*

> ALL THE BROKEN PIECES OF YOUR LIFE, ARE NOTHING MORE THAN A BEAUTIFUL MOSAIC OF YOUR FUTURE.

power of life and death, and those who love it will eat its fruit."

(I know now why so many marriages end in divorce. Spouses pronounce death over each other. Just listen to what husbands and wives say about each other! Surely we shall all eat the fruits of our words. A woman recently said to me, "My husband will never serve God!" Sadly, only I realized what she was pronouncing.)

We went to ICU and took turns standing outside Aldo's glass cage, all the while speaking life over him. Whenever one of us would take a break, the other would take over. The ICU personnel found it strange that we continued to speak life over Aldo, because they really did expect the worst. Aldo's prognosis wasn't good. In days to come I could tell who of the staff had children of their own and who didn't. There were those who cared and those who were simply doing their jobs.

It was a dark time in our lives. The pieces of our clay tablet had cut deeply into our flesh and we were bleeding profusely.

God gave us His Spirit to help us with everthing that we struggle with. We will sacrifice ourselves to God.
I love you Mommy.
God sent me back to tell the world that Jesus lives!
We have to be obedient and speak life! Mommy, please will you always be obedient and do what Jesus shows you to do?

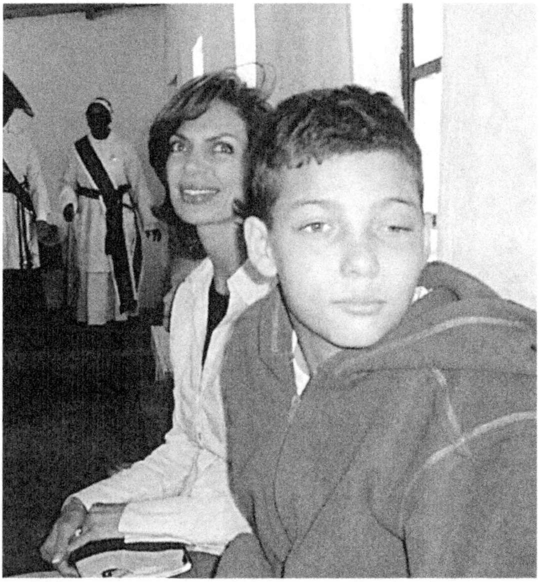

IN THE THRONE ROOM

With the second week, came the second brain operation. They wanted to drain some of the blood that had accumulated and caused pressure on the brain. After this, they would start to wean Aldo off life support to see if he would breathe on his own and live.

The day before the operation, a woman came to see us at the hospital. Love radiated from her face. "I'm a prophetess," she said. I looked at her in disbelief and quickly answered that we were fine and didn't need help. I was skeptical of course. What did I know about prophetesses anyway? She wasn't offended and assured me that she only wanted to pray with me. By the end of the night however, I wanted to be as close to her as I could get, simply because I couldn't resist the love of Jesus that was just radiating from her.

Her name was Terthia.* She asked me if I believed that God could save my child's life and heal him. I had to admit that I didn't *really* believe it, because I'd been listening to the medical experts and was focused on Aldo's prognosis. Terthia told me about a Nigerian pastor who came back from the dead after being in the morgue for four days. Again I was skeptical. If that were true it would surely have made the front pages of every newspaper. She just smiled and assured me that it was true and that I would hear it from the pastor himself at some point in the future. She asked me if I believed that all things were possible with God (Mt. 19:26).

Then we prayed together. She specifically asked me to give my life to God.

> It was like a bell going off somewhere. It had been the third time God had asked me for my life.

She told me that there were things in my life that I needed to confess, because they were a barrier between God and me. At first I was confused and taken aback. I didn't know what I had to confess. God had shown her I had done some fire walking. I was shocked that she knew about it. I had done it, against my better

*Not her real name.

judgement, at a congress. She also said that I was bitter towards my husband for what had happened. Although I had given the devil an opportunity to attack us by fearing and speaking the accident, I had blamed Tinus for it.

I also had to confess my own feelings of guilt regarding the accident. Terthia assured me that the accident was neither Tinus' nor my fault. She explained that the enemy was trying to steal our very lives, because he realized what a special plan God had with our lives. "There is a battle raging in the spiritual realm for Aldo's life, because God has placed a calling on his life," said Terthia. She would return the next day so that we could have communion.

After Terthia left, I remained at Aldo's bedside, until midnight when I too went to bed, trying to get some rest before the next day's operation. I woke up at two a.m. to the sound of a roaring lion running loose in the hallways of the hospital. The sound of its roaring was terrifying and its fury filled my head. I wasn't on any medication and I was definitely *not* hallucinating; it was real. It was the unmistakable sound of a roaring lion. I got up and ran to ICU, where the staff was scurrying around frantically. Although they often battle for life in ICU, even I could sense that this was something else. The lion was still roaring powerfully. The sisters around Aldo's bed looked surprised to see me there and I realized that they would never believe that I'd heard a lion roaring in ICU. They told me later that Terthia had come back and prayed for Aldo while I was sleeping. The alarms and monitors were going off non-stop while she prayed for him. At once I realized that the Lion of Judah had battled against the roaring lion for my son's life, and He had won. Some time, later when I read Rev. 5:5: *"Do not weep! See the Lion of the tribe of Judah, the Root of David has triumphed…"*, I finally understood that God also called me to defeat the roaring lion when He spoke to me on the beach many months before.

I stayed with Aldo until the doctors came in to see him. The operation only took place in the afternoon and it became a long and exhausting day. Aldo came out of the theatre and I was told to phone Tinus so that he could come to the hospital. They were going to wean Aldo off the morphine. When they switched off the first life support machines, Aldo's heart rate was very slow. It was excruciating. I had reached my breaking point.

I went into my hospital room and pulled my coat over my head. And then I prayed. I was desperate for God and called to Him with everything in me. For the first time in my life, I prayed "in spirit and in truth" (Jn. 4:23) and immediately God answered me in a voice that I could hear and said, *"Take the shoes from your feet, because you're standing on holy ground".* Just like with Moses, I thought.

"Retha, do you believe that my Son's sacrifice was perfect and complete?" He asked, knowing that I didn't fully understand the blood of Jesus.

"Yes, Lord."

He asked me the exact same question again, but before I could answer, I relived the crucifixion. I saw Him taking my punishment. After each blow that He would receive, God's voice said, "I did it for you, Retha". And then He quoted John 3:16 exactly: "*For God so loved the world, that he gave his one and only Son that whoever believes in him shall not perish, but have eternal life.*"

After Jesus had taken the 39 blows, darkness came. I saw Jesus hanging on the cross. I heard Him calling out in pain. I knew then that it wasn't the pain from the beating, or the nails through His hands, but the pain of carrying the sins of the world and being cut off from the Father that made Him cry out.

When Jesus died, I saw the curtain in the temple being torn from top to bottom. Then God invited me into the Holy of holies, "Come into My presence, My child." I saw thousands of people in the forecourt as I passed through it and went into the Most Holy Place. Standing in His presence, He told me to strip off all the masks I'd been wearing. "I'm not interested in your pretences or your good works," God said, "I want your life." Suddenly I could see how I'd been hiding behind the masks of perfectionism, pride, jealously, self-loathing, self-pity, frustration and aggression. In that moment I saw myself as from the outside: I saw Retha, the gossip; Retha, the closed book; Retha, the achiever who cannot stand failure. God wanted my life, not my works, but how to do it. "Help me to lay down my life, Lord," I pleaded.

Then I saw a wash-bowl in front of me. It was filled with the blood of Jesus and I knew I had to be cleansed by it. Nothing but the blood of Jesus can free us from the Law. God told me that I was in the Most Holy Place. I had to embrace the Truth, and confess my sin. When God forgives us, He removes our sin from us as far as the East is removed from the West (Ps. 103:12).

In my mind's eye I saw myself entering the blood. When I emerged from it, there was no condemnation for me anymore (Rom. 8:1). Since then, I've learnt that a Jewish bride has to go through a ritual bath, called

> I UNDERSTOOD GOD'S MESSAGE THEN: NO MATTER WHO YOU ARE, OR WHAT YOU'VE DONE IN YOUR LIFE, THE BLOOD OF JESUS MAKES YOU PURE AND NEW – WHITER THAN THE SNOW.

the "*mikva*". Even if she's no longer a virgin, she is considered cleansed and made holy by the "*mikva*".

He cleansed me from all sin, my pride and my self-importance. He can do it for you too.

I had to be filled with the Holy Spirit if I wanted to enter the Holy of holies. "Lord, do you remember how many Sundays I stood in church, asking to be filled with the Spirit," I asked.

"It was impossible then," He answered. "You were too full of yourself. There was no room for My Spirit. Only once you've died unto yourself, can you be filled with My Spirit." I now understand why Paul says he dies unto himself every day (Gal. 2:20).

Again God called me into the Holy of holies. In this Most Holy Place Spirit speaks to spirit. It's *"deep unto deep"* (Ps. 42:7). Here there are no words. Only tears and joy and life! After 40 years, and in a hospital room, with my coat pulled over my head, I finally met God face to face.

On one side of the hospital hall, my child was fighting for his life and on the other side of the hall, I was meeting God. It changed one of the worst days of my life into one of the best. I had found what I'd always been searching for: Jesus. And He is enough. In that moment I didn't care whether Aldo lived or died, or whether I lived or died. Rom. 14:8 says: *"So, whether we live or die, we belong to the Lord,"* and I understood it for the first time. I wanted to shout with joy! I wanted the world to know, "The Lion of Judah is in me. We are one!"

I was in the awesome presence of God and I could bask in His prefect love. What an indescribable love! It's a love that I will never comprehend. Sitting at the throne of God, there is fire and warmth. All my needs and desires were fulfilled in His presence. In a single instant I experienced total acceptance, grace and peace. God is the answer! Every day I meet people who are desperate to find these gifts. But the blessing isn't in these gifts. It's in the One who gives them.

> INSTEAD OF LOOKING FOR THE GIFTS, WE SHOULD SEEK OUT THE GIFT GIVER. WE NEED GOD, AND GOD ALONE.

"Come to the throne of grace so that I can give you grace" – (Heb. 4:16). Persevere until you're in the presence of the Lord; until you're in the Holy of holies.

In His presence, in that Most Holy Place, I saw a blinding light. That's because God is Light and in Him there is no darkness. I was basking in this light when He asked me, "Retha are you willing to sacrifice your child?"

The question caught me off guard. For 10 years Aldo had been my only child; my life! I didn't understand what God was trying to say. Did He really want my child to die after everything we'd been through?

"Are you willing to put your child on the altar and sacrifice him?" asked God again. Before I could answer, Mt. 10:37 came to me, *"...anyone who loves his son or daughter more than me, is not worthy of me"*.

I knew immediately that the Holy Spirit was deliberately reminding me of this Scripture because God was speaking seriously and directly to me about my idealized view of Aldo. I had great dreams for him; I almost lived his life *for* him. I instantly knew that the priorities in our house were skew, as I suspect they are in most people's lives. Our children come first, then our marriages, our jobs and only then, God.

> SURELY, GOD SHOULD COME FIRST, THEN OUR MARRIAGES, OUR CHILDREN, AND ONLY THEN, OUR JOBS.

I knew without a doubt that I had to place Aldo on the altar. I would sacrifice him, not because I had to, but because I wanted to.

In my spirit, I saw Aldo lying on a bench. God told me to leave him there. I could see God's extended hands and I heard His comforting voice. He spoke softly to me, telling me that Aldo didn't belong to me anymore. God had a wonderful plan for Aldo. He would heal him and Aldo would tell the world that Jesus is alive. It sounded strange to me. My child, no God's child, would tell the world that Jesus is alive!

God showed me that I needed faith. I had to hope against all hope. In Heb. 6 I found an example of this hope. Abraham had to keep the faith that he would have descendants although both he and Sara were long past their childbearing age. It seemed humanly impossible, but he held fast to God's promise. I decided there and then, that even if it looked like there was no hope for Aldo, I would keep hoping, because to hope, is to have faith.

It was as if God was saying that without my faith, His promise to heal Aldo would be meaningless. My faith was needed for the miracle to happen. In Mt. 9:20-22 we read about the woman who suffered from bleeding for 12 years. She believed that once she touched Jesus, she would be healed. It was her faith that caused the healing to take place, not Jesus' garment! That day, I too touched the Almighty and I know that the miracle took place immediately in the spiritual realm. It's only a matter of time before it manifests itself here, in the physical realm. God was saying, "Life on Earth is not about you, Retha. It's all about Me. The glory is Mine."

"Lord, You don't understand," I thought, "Today *is* about me. It's *my* child and *my* pain. I'm sitting among the pieces of my clay tablet and they are cutting deeply into my flesh."

"I'm aware of your pain and suffering," God answered. "But even your pain and suffering is about Me. I AM the center of everything that is, was and shall be. Relinquish control of your life. I'm the Ruler of your life, not you."

When I finally opened my eyes, one-and-a-half-hour had passed. In ICU they'd stopped all the pain medication and had switched off the life support machines. Aldo's heart rate had accelerated and he was gnashing his teeth.

> GOD HAD STEPPED IN AND A MIRACLE WAS UNFOLDING IN FRONT OF MY VERY EYES.

I returned to my room, and cried. The prophetess returned. I asked her to explain the blood-covenant experience that I'd just had with God. She said it was much like the covenant that God had made with Abraham after God had asked him to sacrifice his son. She reminded me of Gen. 22:8. It reads, *"... God himself will provide the lamb for the burnt offering my son..."*.

Terthia told me that a great battle had raged for my son's life the night before. But the war had been won. It was a strange concept for me to grasp. She told me that God had woken her and told her to return to the hospital to pray for Aldo, because there was a battle for his life. She returned to Aldo's bedside and continued to pray for him. She could sense something like a black funnel circling around his bed. The prophetess then prayed for a wall of fire around Aldo's bed and over his life. "In the end the enemy was defeated and fled roaring like a lion in the hospital hallways," she said. There definitely is a spiritual dimension and it's where the devil goes round like a roaring lion looking for those that he can devour (1 Pet. 5:8).

FIGHTING IN FAITH

The road to recovery would be a long one. Although Aldo had survived the accident, he was still in a coma and his future was unsure. Still God promises that He will finish the good work that He has started.

In the first month after the accident, Aldo came off all life support. His right eye started moving, but the left eye remained motionless and the doctors said he would be blind in that eye. He was transferred to a normal recovery ward.

He couldn't speak, because of the trachea in his throat. His little body was still very stiff and immobile. After the second month, the doctors referred us to institutions where they care for children who are mentally retarded or who had suffered severe brain injuries. The prognosis was that Aldo would never sit, stand or walk unaided. He would be dependent on others for all his motor functions for the rest of his life. Every time when we received this kind of bad news about Aldo, a great silence would fall between Tinus and me.

I started praying for Aldo's body then, commanding it to align itself with God's will and Word. It's not His will that we should suffer or remain ill. I stood firm on Lk. 4:18-19: *"... he has sent me to proclaim freedom for the prisoners, and recovery of sight for the blind, to release the oppressed, to proclaim the year of the Lord's favor".* Every time some negative news was pronounced over Aldo, I cancelled it in Jesus' name. I continued to proclaim that no weapon formed against us shall prosper (Is. 54:17). I just had to keep hoping; believing in things that I couldn't yet see (Heb. 11:1). I had to have faith. It was one of the hardest things I've ever had to do in my life. Whenever someone would ask how we were doing, I'd say, "We are fighting the good fight in faith!"

Finally some good news! The doctor who examined Aldo's shoulder exclaimed, "Mrs. McPherson, this is a miracle!" I felt like jumping up and down and screaming with joy, even if he was only talking about Aldo's shoulder. God is good and even medical experts are starting to admit it nowadays.

Aldo was transferred to a hospital in Pretoria (Gauteng), from where we finally took him home. We'd decided that if Aldo needed care, we would be the ones giving it. We hired day- and night nursing staff to help us.

Aldo's mouth was static. His jaws were contorted

to the side and he couldn't open his mouth at all. He was fed through a feeding tube that was inserted in his stomach. I knew what God had told me: Aldo would tell the world that Jesus is alive! I hadn't shared this promise with anyone, because I knew they wouldn't understand the experience I had had with God. I also didn't know that Aldo knew about everything that had happened between God and me.

Being convinced that Aldo would regain the use of his mouth, I wanted to force open his jaws so that he could talk. We tried everything, but with no success.

We went back to the surgeon to find out if there was anything we could do to get him to open his mouth. He told us that we were lucky. Lucky, that Aldo's jaws weren't stuck in an open gaping position. Children who sustained the type of brain injury Aldo had, had one of two reactions. Either the child would have a clenched jaw, like Aldo did, or the mouth could be stuck in a perpetual wide-open contorted yawn. The doctor illustrated his point by pulling an awful face, opening his mouth as wide as he could and tilting his head, saying "Ahhh". Aldo was seated between Tinus and I directly in front of this insensitive man who repeatedly illustrated his point this way. It was all the more upsetting because he was doing it in front of Aldo, I thought. Didn't he realize that Aldo could hear and understand every word he said? It was a bitter pill to swallow and I had to fight back my tears. Then from somewhere inside me came a little bit of humor. I remember thinking, "Dear Lord, spare this man. For if the bell should toll for him now, surely his face would be stuck in this position forever." The doctor sent us home with the assurance that Aldo would not open his mouth... not ever.

I cried all the way home. I didn't want to accept it.

We tried a different doctor and insisted that he inject Aldo's jaws so that he could open his mouth.

The doctor, realizing that we were desperate, injected Aldo, but when Aldo came out of the theatre that night, his jaws were still shut. The sympathetic doctor couldn't give us any hope. He didn't even give us a prescription!

Still, I wouldn't believe it. At home, I took my Bible and started talking to God in earnest. I claimed the promise in Mk. 11:24: *"Therefore I tell you, whatever you ask for in prayer, believe that you have received it, and it will be yours."* My tears stained my Bible. I pleaded with God and reminded Him of His promise that Aldo would tell the world that Jesus lives. I told Him that I didn't care how He did it. He is the Creator of heaven and earth, and I refuse to believe that Aldo's jaws will remain shut. (Please remember that I hadn't become holy after my spiritual encounter with God. I wasn't some kind of passive puppet. I battled daily with my sinful, human nature. I still do.)

I agued with God. I told Him that I was holding Him to His Word. I declared that when I had sacrificed Aldo that day, and surrendered control of my life, I stopped reacting to my emotions. I wouldn't be ruled by, or believe the pronouncements the world made regarding Aldo either. I kept on confessing His Word. I couldn't do anything else, since God Himself, had said it. I confessed my own weakness and inability and pleaded for God's power over me. I trusted God.

God replied with one Scripture – Jn. 6:53-56: *"... I tell you the truth, unless you eat the flesh of the Son of Man and drink this blood, you have no life in you. Whoever eats my flesh and drinks my blood has eternal life and I will raise him up at the last day. For my flesh is real food and my blood is real drink. Whoever eats my flesh and drinks my blood remains in me, and I in him."*

I had to take communion. I must have eaten loaves of bread with God in those days! Whenever I was in the kitchen, I would break off a piece of bread and confess that I died with Jesus, and when I took a sip of juice, I confessed that I was resurrected with Him too.

> IT'S ONE THING TO DIE WITH CHRIST, BUT IT'S QUITE ANOTHER TO BE RESURRECTED WITH HIM.

Very few people actually succeed in *living* with Him. In Jn. 14:6 the Bible tells us that Jesus is the Truth, the Way and *the Life*. I repeat, Jesus came so that we may have *life*, and have it to the full!

We have to *live* for and with Christ. It is our covenant and calling. This is what I had to stand on. And I stand on it still! Eating the bread means I choose to *live* with Jesus, dying to myself and my own agenda. It's not some kind of dead doctrine. God has taught me to honor the blood covenant of communion and to trust Him with my life.

I practiced communion daily and kept looking for changes in Aldo. At that stage he couldn't even move. He was just lying there. I remained positive and took communion whenever I could, always choosing to live with Jesus. I refused to sit among the pieces of my broken clay tablet.

> God wants to be your first love again. God wants to bless you so that you can speak life and proclaim His Word. Be holy, like He wants you to be. May God use us as He sees fit. Anoint me, Mommy, and tell the world that Jesus is alive.

TURNING THE TIDE

One day things started to change. I often compare it to what is described in Ezek. 47:1- 6, where the prophet sees the water flowing out of the temple. At first the water is a only trickle, then it becomes ankle-deep. It rises to his knees and then becomes waist-deep. Finally in verse 5 we read: *"but now it was a river that I could not cross, because the water had risen and was deep enough to swim in – a river that no one could cross."*

In my life too, I could feel that the

water was rising. The Spirit became stronger as I denounced my sinful flesh. I'm reminded that Jesus is coming back for a bride who has conquered the flesh. We have to live by the Spirit. And so my personal goals changed. I wanted the words of Ps. 1:3 to apply to me: *"He is like a tree planted by streams of water, which yields its fruit in season and whose leaf does not wither; Whatever he does prospers."*

I have come to realize that I can only bear fruit if the immortal seed of God is implanted in my heart. That seed is implanted in your heart when you confess, "Lord, I'm done. I can't go on any further." God is *not* in control if you're still trying to get things done in your own power. Then *you* are in control. God will not compete with you for control of your life. No, we have to lay down everything at God's feet, then step back and wait for Him to do the work.

Now that I've become one with the living God, He has become the most important One. I only exist in and through Him. I don't have to do anything. He accomplishes everything. This very book is an example of this. I had no idea how to go about writing a book, but I thank God that I didn't have to. I'm not the one writing it, after all, God is. I also thank God that I don't have to worry about the future, or about providing for my family or even concern myself about Aldo's future. God is in control. I'm merely an instrument in His hand. Because Jesus died on the cross for me, I have the victory.

Things may seem hopeless when we look at them with fleshly eyes: Aldo still hobbles about and falls down often. Seen through human eyes, he's clearly not 100% normal, and his speech is very slow and monotone, but I've been set free. I don't have to do it on my own. God says in Phil. 1:6 that He will finish what He has started. Whatever God has started within you, He will complete it too, if you'll allow Him to do it.

It had been months and Aldo still couldn't open his mouth. Even if I addressed him directly, he would only stare back at me. On my way to Cape Town (Western Cape), I passed by *Sweets from Heaven* at the airport. "Their worms are the sourest ones that you can get anywhere," Aldo used to say. I always bought him sour worms at the airport when I traveled. Walking into the store that day, I felt that everyone knew my child couldn't eat them. Although I usually bought a bag full of worms, I only took four worms that day, paid for them and went home. But at home I wanted to hide the worms in my cupboard. I felt uncomfortable buying sweets for Aldo who couldn't eat anything, let alone sweets! I spoke to God: "Why did I buy these sour worms?"

I can't explain it, but I felt that God wanted me to squeeze those sour worms into Aldo's cheeks, under his teeth. Although I knew he couldn't swallow, and therefore couldn't get anything in his throat, I went ahead and squeezed one sour worm into his jaw every day, for four consecutive days.

After the fourth day, Aldo opened his mouth.

I cried with pure joy! I shouted and I screamed. I realized that if I hadn't obeyed God, Aldo's jaws would have remained shut. Sometimes, you just know that the voice you're hearing inside of you is God's voice. If I had listened to reason and caution, I would have never forced that first worm in his jaw.

> MY GOD IS A SUPERNATURAL GOD! NOTHING IS IMPOSSIBLE WITH HIM! SOMETIMES HE DELIBERATELY WORKS AGAINST LOGIC, SO THAT WE CAN KNOW THAT HE IS ALMIGHTY.

After this breakthrough, we worked out a diet for Aldo, which included avocado and other soft foods. We started feeding him small pieces of real food. The first thing I put into Aldo's mouth after he'd opened it, was a tiny piece of bread. I also put a few drops of juice on his lips and he swallowed it eagerly. We took communion together. One drop of Jesus' blood is enough for me. And it is enough for Aldo's healing too.

When we brought Aldo home, he was blind in one eye, while the other one remained closed and motionless. Even so, he had started writing and continued with home schooling. At night he slept in our room on a mattress, since we feared that he might fall off his bed, if he slept in his own room, some distance away from us. We were no longer using nappies, and thus we had to carry Aldo to the bathroom during the night.

Aldo woke me up one night. "Mom, did you see Jesus?" he asked. I told him that I hadn't seen Him, but that I had just been dreaming about Him. Aldo was adamant that Jesus had just been in the room and had touched his eye.

"Can you see, Aldo?" I asked excitedly. He shook his head. I switched off the light again and told him that we had to get some sleep. But I didn't sleep. I pressed my face into the pillow and cried. Although there were no tears, my spirit was sobbing. "God, I need a miracle," I cried.

"No Retha, you need faith" came the soft, loving reply.

It was so hard. The emotional pain was excruciating.

Some two weeks later I returned home quite late, after speaking in Nelspruit (Limpopo). Aldo was already asleep in our room. His blind eye was closed, but the static one was open. I didn't find it strange, since we had to put salve in that eye every night and close it for him. I thought that Tinus had just forgotten to do it.

Due to the injury to the mid-brain, Aldo had a hard time falling asleep. Even now he has to take an herbal sleeping tablet every night so that he can get some rest. There were nights when we didn't get any sleep at all. We would see the sun rising, without having slept a wink. God taught me to be patient during those times when the tears and tiredness became too much to bear. Sometimes Aldo would start screaming from utter exhaustion and there was nothing I could do to help him. Those nights forged a very strong bond between my son and I. Anointing him with oil worked at times, but sometimes, nothing could keep him from screaming with frustration and anger at not being able to sleep.

So when I saw Aldo sleeping that night, I sat down next to him and started praying for him in my spirit. Before getting up to fetch the salve for his eye, I formed a kiss with my mouth, but because I didn't want to wake him, I didn't dare touch him with my lips. I was surprised to see him forming a kiss in return.

"Aldo, could you see me just now?" I asked.

He gave me the thumbs up. "I told you He was here."

We took Aldo back to the eye specialist. He said that Aldo had recovered his sight in that eye completely. God had done another miracle! Today, Aldo's eyelid still droops and that impacts negatively on his balance and reading ability, but his eyes move simultaneously now, which hadn't been the case when his sight was just restored. After two additional surgeries to lift the eyelid failed, the doctor told us to accept it. Aldo was very upset and exclaimed, "You don't know my Jesus!"

We went to a different specialist for a second opinion, and he encouraged us. So much of the nerve damage had been reversed that he concluded it had to be God's work. God's time is not my time.

When you see Aldo, you might think that I'm expecting too much; that I want the impossible. But I assure you it *is* possible. I too didn't know what the future held for Aldo when he was lying in a coma in that hospital bed. I didn't know if he would even survive it. Today I know that I don't have to worry anymore, because I don't have to do anything. It is not *my* work. It's God's work and He will finish it. And He will do it perfectly. Aldo's progress to date has nothing to do with me. It certainly is not because of who, or what I am, nor due to anything that I have done. All I have to do is keep the faith.

MESSENGER FROM GOD

When we first brought Aldo home, he had little control over his muscles and didn't move a lot. He would just lie there, staring at us. We decided that he had to get some exercise to keep his muscles from going limp, so we put him on a stationary bike. But it was easier said than done. Two people had to keep his body in an upright position on the bike, and another one had to hold up his head, while two more people had to turn the pedals, to which Aldo's feet were fastened.

We must have looked a sight! People were confounded that we went to so much trouble for a child who would never walk again. Never walk again? This child will tell the world that Jesus lives!

In order for Aldo to resume his education at home, he had to learn the alphabet from scratch. So we fastened him to a chair, using bandages and the occupational therapist came to our house and retaught him the alphabet. One day, he stared intently at a pen. I asked him if he wanted to write. He nodded ever so slightly. It was a definite "Yes". I put the pen in his hand and held his wrist, because the muscles in his right hand jerks randomly. He started writing:

> Thanks for what you did for me. Mom, if you hadn't sacrificed me, I'd be dead now!

I was completely dumbfounded. "How do you know about that?" I screamed. He wrote down his reply:

> Remember after the accident when you bent over me? You looked directly into Jesus' eyes when He came to pick me up and take me to heaven. I was in heaven with Him all the time. He taught me everything in heaven. He taught me His Word.

I was amazed to hear this. I immediately got his suitcase, (Would you believe that after four months, his lunch box was still inside!) took out his math book and presented him with a fraction. He promptly wrote down the answer. I scolded him for not showing his calculations, but he again wrote down only the answer. I wasn't sure about the correct answer myself, and so I quickly phoned Tinus to find out if it was in fact correct. He confirmed that it was.

I was over the moon. We were told that Aldo wouldn't remember the accident or things that happened before it, but Aldo had proven them all wrong. God had proven the world wrong. I always knew my child was still inside this broken little body!

I phoned the doctor, who wouldn't believe that Aldo would be healed, and told him to plug in his fax, because I was sending him the calculation that Aldo had just done! Later I regretted my actions. My motives weren't pure. I was angry at the doctor for not having faith. I guess he was only doing his job and based his predictions on the medical facts of Aldo's case. I had wanted to prove him wrong. Instead of allowing the Holy Spirit to convince the doctor that Jesus is alive, I had wanted to prove it to him. I have since had to confess this and ask forgiveness for having judged him. Only then could I also forgive the doctor.

Aldo remembered everything, even the accident itself. Months later, when we were on our way to the airport one day, Aldo started telling us in detail how his spirit had left his body at the crash site. He says it felt like a grey matter leaving his body and the next moment his body was complete and without blemish. "I was completely healed," he said. "I saw you guys kneeling down next to me. I saw everything."

Aldo wrote every day. I remember how he would write "Jesus" and encircle it. He wrote continuously, filling pages upon pages. I didn't understand it and so I asked him why he did it.

> Thank you Jesus that I will talk; that I will walk.

"Do you remember the dream when you had to speak life over me? Jesus also told me to speak life every day, and that is what I'm doing."

Then came a request we didn't expect or understand. He turned the page that he was writing on sideways and wrote: "Will you let me be baptized?" I found it odd since he was baptized as a baby. I tried talking him out of it, but Aldo insisted on it and wouldn't talk about anything else. Finally I asked him why it was so important to him. He wrote:

> Jesus said I have to be baptized as soon as I get back. And we have to be obedient, Mommy.

I realized then that this must be a command from God. We certainly never discussed adult baptizm with him. I phoned our Reverend, who was in Jerusalem at the time, and told him about it. Then I took Aldo to church where someone from the congregation lifted him out of his wheelchair and into the water in the bath. When Aldo was baptized his one little eye was shining like never before. After the baptizm, Aldo repeatedly wrote,

> Thank you for being obedient to God. It is what all people should do. When God speaks, we have to obey Him, Mommy.

About a month after his baptizm, Aldo was floating on a tube in the pool when a friend of mine came to visit. When he saw her, he made a sound as if to call her over to him. He indicated that he wanted to write and so I handed him the clipboard and a pen. This is what he wrote:

> Ma'am, Jesus says you have to be baptized. He says He has been speaking to you about it for a long time now, but you don't want to listen. Now is the time to do it.

I was really embarrassed and didn't want to show her the letter, but she insisted. I handed it over and she read it. Then she burst into tears, saying that Aldo was right. God had been speaking to her about being baptized for months now. She got into the pool there and then and Aldo baptized her.

Aldo started writing more and more about heaven. I didn't know what to make of it, so I spoke to God, "Lord, the things that my child writes are so unbelievable, so supernatural. I don't understand it. How could he have been in heaven?" He answered me with Jn. 11:40: *"Did I not tell you that if you believed, you would see the glory of God?"*

> We will see God in heaven, along with all the angels and other people like Abraham and Moses. Anton and Dwane will also be there. I'm excited about going back to heaven. Aren't you? Sometimes, when I'm being difficult it is just because I really want to go back there. Mommy, please tell all the people that they will either go to heaven or to hell. Those who obey the devil will go to hell, but God's children, who live the way He wants us to live, will go to heaven. You and I will see Jesus together, Mommy. I'm so looking forward to that.

One day, Aldo wrote: Jesus said, we will not be disappointed, because He lives. We just have to stand fast in faith. Thank You, Jesus.

It was hard to accept the fact that our son was now a messenger from God and even harder to deal with his acute awareness of his connection to the Spirit and to his assignment. Although Aldo couldn't yet speak to the world, his ministry was very effective in our house.

> I write only what the Holy Spirit tells me to write.

The day when Aldo started calling out for someone named Anton, I was really confused. Aldo could only say a few words at that stage, but he kept calling out for Anton. We didn't even know anyone by that name! I thought he just needed a change of scenery and so I took him to a shopping mall, but he kept calling, "Anton, Anton". That night he wrote that he had met Anton in heaven. "You have to tell his mother and father that he is healthy now." When Aldo said this, he made a circular motion around his head that I didn't understand at the time. Then he drew directions for me to get to the house where Anton's parents lived. But instead of going to look for them, I placed it in the file where I kept all his other letters. Truth be told, I never planned on looking for them.

One day when a friend of mine was visiting, Aldo wrote her a note saying I was being disobedient to God.

> Mom has to look for Anton's parents. She has to tell them that he is healthy and happy with Jesus.

My friend took the directions that Aldo gave me and went looking for Anton's parents. She found them and delivered Aldo's message. It turns out that Anton had Down's syndrome and that is what Aldo tried to indicate when he made the circle around his head. Anton was everything Aldo had said and looked just like he had described him.

Aldo also met Dwane in heaven. Early one morning Aldo wrote, "Mom, do you remember those people whose son suffocated in the sand?" I did remember them for they contacted and supported us while Aldo was in a coma in hospital. I didn't understand how Aldo knew about them though. He wrote them a letter:

> Dwane is safe with Jesus in heaven. He doesn't want to come back, but he wants you to be ready.

When God spoke to me again, He asked me how Jesus was born. I could only answer that it had been supernatural. Supernatural – just like Aldo's letters from God. There were days when all Aldo wrote was:

> Believe in God. Believe in God.

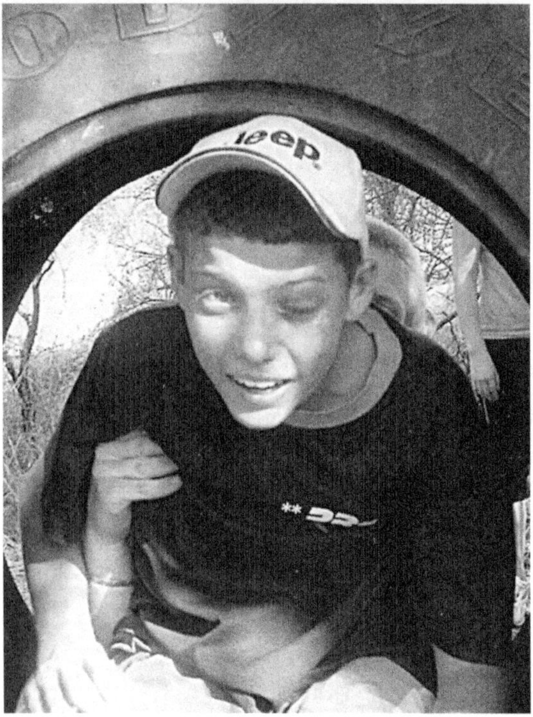

FINDING A NEW VOICE

I came home from town one day, feeling bruised. Someone had asked me when I was going to wake up and realize that Aldo wasn't going to get better. Aldo looked into my eyes and asked: "When God returns, will He find even one person who still believes in Him?"

My life had become a strange journey. Where I had once paid Aldo R5 for every five minutes in which said nothing, just to have a little peace and quiet on the trip between Pretoria and Hartebeespoort, I would've paid any amount just to hear him chatting away after the accident. Our little chatterbox was silent. Many days it was all I could do to plead with God to have mercy on me; to help me keep the faith.

We'd been to many speech therapists, but they all concurred: Aldo would never speak again. I had to hold on to God's promise that Aldo would tell the world that Jesus is alive! But it was hard. After showing Aldo's X-rays to yet another therapist, Aldo wanted to know what she said. I just couldn't tell him and so I said that her schedule was too full and therefore she couldn't help us.

After I had testified on a radio broadcast, a speech therapist contacted me. God had convinced her to help Aldo. I took Aldo to see her, but when we arrived, she seemed hesitant. Aldo wrote her a note saying she should relax, since Jesus Himself would make him speak. Every day he wrote:

> Jesus will make me speak.

For months no sound passed over Aldo's lips, but she kept encouraging him to make sounds, because sounds would eventually become words. At a session one day, I just told him to say the word "caterpillar" for her. He opened his mouth and said "Cat - er- pil – lar". And suddenly he was talking.

Today, Aldo speaks reasonably clearly albeit somewhat monotone. The journey to this point where I can hear and understand him, has taught me again, that my time is not God's time.

To his friends, who had prayed for him, he writes this note:

Jesus saved my life. He wants to use our lives to His honor. We have to honor Him. Thank you all for praying for me. Jesus told me that you were praying for me. He was so proud of you, because you trusted Him. He loves you all a lot. We have to make Him happy by serving Him. He wants to bless us and anoint us with His Holy Spirit. We will all stand in front of His throne one day.

Aldo's letters gave me hope. In one of them he wrote that his mother covers him with love; she knows that he is going to be healed because she was with him in the throne room with God when Jesus promised that He would heal him. He adds that Jesus has already paid the price for his healing and that we mustn't stop believing.

Aldo writes that he and I will sacrifice each other to God continuously and testify to the world about Jesus because, and this he writes in large letters,

"the world has to hear that Jesus is alive!"

In yet another letter, Aldo writes Jesus says accidents happen because we are still living *in* the world. He says Tinus and I shouldn't blame ourselves for what happened, because Jesus says that we will glorify His name through it.

Even though Aldo hadn't attended school for six months in 2004, he still passed his exams at the end of the year with flying colors. A remarkable achievement since he couldn't write unassisted and could only speak a word here and there! We engaged a teacher and Aldo received home schooling for the next year. However, when she resigned after that year, I didn't know if or where we would ever find another teacher to take over Aldo's education. It may sound as if we had everything under control when I talk about Aldo, but it wasn't easy to teach him. The fact remained that he had sustained a brain injury and we had to deal with everything that that entails.

During our annual holiday, I prayed constantly about what we should do regarding Aldo's education. Few people could understand Aldo when he spoke, and I realized that whoever would take over Aldo's care, would have to be very special indeed; almost supernatural. She would have to be an angel! Still in my spirit, I knew that I needn't worry about it. God was in control of that situation too.

Back home, the perfect woman for the job was referred to us. I saw the love of Jesus in her eyes the minute she set foot in the door. She was the answer to my prayers. She'd previously been a remedial teacher, and had told God the year before that she desired to work with children again. She'd even followed Aldo's story in the news when it happened and she told me how thrilled she'd been to read about his progress. When she'd read the stories in the papers, she didn't know that she would play a major part in

God's plan for Aldo's life.

And so Patricia, or Patrys as we call her, became Aldo's teacher. She always treats him with lots of love and kindness even when he is moody and difficult and she's supported us during the times when he relapsed and was very ill. Whenever I would ask her how Aldo was doing, her answer would always be that he was doing very well. She too speaks life and keeps the faith. To me, Patrys is a living example of 1 Cor. 13:13: *"And now these three remain: faith, hope and love. But the greatest of these is love."*

Aldo often sees and talks to angels. But when someone recently asked him what an angel looked like, he wrote that whoever wanted to see an angel on Earth, need only look at his teacher. When I read this in his journal, I cried. Perhaps other people wouldn't understand it, but to us, Patrys truly *is* an angel sent by God to bless us. Miss Patrys is Aldo's guardian angel. In addition to taking him to his therapy every day, she protects him, cares for him, teaches him and disciplines him. She guides him on his way.

Thank You Lord for Patrys!

One night in September 2006, Aldo went missing from the house. When Tinus got up around three a.m. to take him to the bathroom, he couldn't find him anywhere. He woke me up and we started looking for our son. I remember still making a joke about the rapture having taken place. Tinus wasn't amused. We finally found Aldo on the vacant lot next to our house. He was standing under a tree, talking to someone only he could see.

"Who are you talking to, Aldo?" Tinus enquired.

"Can't you see him?" asked Aldo.

We replied that we didn't see anyone other than him. "It's the angel Raphael," Aldo replied. Because nobody in their right mind wanders around outside at three a.m. in Gauteng Province, we brought Aldo back to the house. Although we told him to stop, Aldo kept on talking. I suppose the angel hadn't yet finished their conversation and because he was still talking, so was Aldo.

"Tell Raphael that you have to go to sleep now, because you have school in the morning," I said, in an attempt to get Aldo to quiet down. But it was impossible. The presence of the angel in our house was simply overpowering. The following day Aldo wrote:

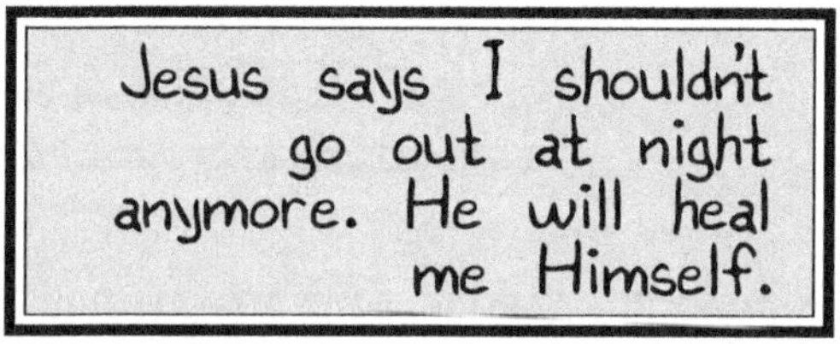
Jesus says I shouldn't go out at night anymore. He will heal me Himself.

The next day I did an Internet search on Raphael. It turns out that he is mentioned in one of the apocryphal books of the Bible as the archangel of healing. He is supposedly one of seven angels who carry the prayers of the righteous and who can enter into the glory of God. It is claimed that Raphael was sent to heal Tobit of blindness and to bind the unclean spirit of Asmodeus, who according to myth, was tasked to destroy marriages.

I prayed to God, asking why only Aldo had encounters with angels. Why didn't I see them too? The only answer that came to me was another prayer: *"Open the eyes of my heart, Lord"* (2 Kgs. 6:17).

I'm frequently invited to testify and people have also asked Aldo to speak, but he isn't ready to do it yet. Although his spirit is like a giant, his body isn't in line with God's will and Word yet. He often writes in his journal that God will perfect the work He has started in him and those are the days when my spirit rejoices, "Jesus is alive!"

In some ways, Aldo is already testifying. He writes almost every day.

> Mommy, tell the world that Jesus lives! I saw Him and Moses and Abraham and the angels. God was seated on His throne and told me to tell the world about Him.

Aldo has the gift of prophecy, but he struggles to express himself coherently. Perhaps I should give an example to explain what I'm trying to say. He once prophesied over one of his school teachers, who'd come to look after him while Patrys handled an urgent matter. The teacher in question had just had a miscarriage and was having a hard time dealing with it. Looking into her eyes, he told her that he saw a golden thread running through them. He told her that she'd have a baby boy on the 11th of October 2006. His message gave her hope and she clung to it in faith. She soon found out that she was indeed pregnant again. Her due date was around November 18, but she believed Aldo's prophecy and ensured that everything was ready for the baby by the 11th of October. On cue, she started having strong contractions on October 11th, and was admitted to hospital. The gynecologist tried to delay the labor, but by the 13th they could no longer inhibit it and her baby boy was born through an emergency C-section on that day. She often testifies that if the doctor hadn't intervened, the baby would have been born on the 11th, just like Aldo had prophesied. God is always 100% accurate.

While I was consulting with a client one day, Aldo came home from school. He looked at the woman who was with me and she looked at him. I immediately knew that if he stared like that, something was about to happen. He took her by the arm and told her that Jesus had sent him back from heaven to tell the world that He is alive. I started apologizing for his behavior, when she smiled broadly and said that she wasn't offended, because she believed in reincarnation.

Reincarnation! I felt sorry for her because I knew that she didn't know the truth. God's Word teaches us in Hos. 4:6 that *"... my people are destroyed from lack of knowledge"*. If she knew the Word, she'd have known the truth written in Heb. 9:27 that people are *"destined to die once, and after that to face judgment"*.

I hope you see what I mean from these two examples. Aldo often has a message for specific people and I believe he has a powerful testimony, but he can't express it in a coherent way, yet.

Aldo identifies with another prophet from the Bible: Samuel. On occasion Aldo wrote that he was like Samuel who had to go back to the temple to study the Scriptures. Samuel returned to the temple when he was 12-years-old and Aldo was 12-years-old when the accident happened. "Mommy, you are like Hanna, from the Bible. She was Samuel's mother. Samuel didn't belong to her and I don't belong to you anymore, Mommy. Remember you sacrificed me to God; I belong to Him now," said Aldo.

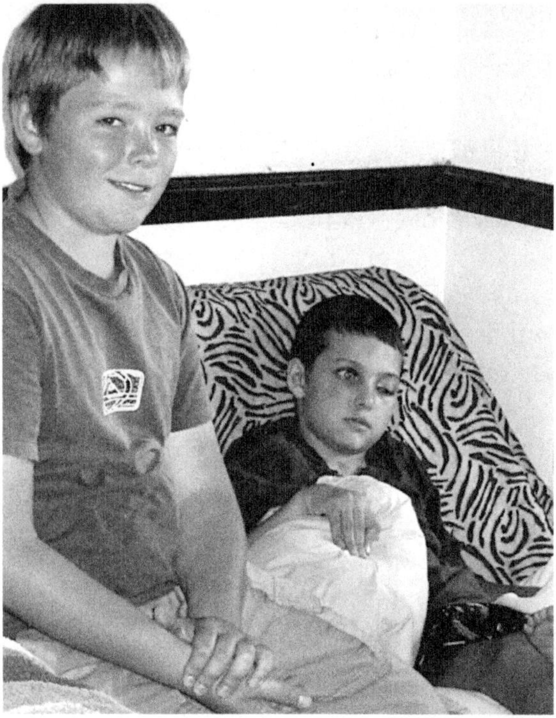

FRIENDSHIP IN HARDSHIP

Before the accident Aldo was in a mainstream school and had lots of friends. Only one of those friends, Bradley, kept calling after the accident. Even when Aldo was in a coma, Bradley was not put off. I remember him coming over to the house when Aldo first came home. Bradley just kept on showing his love. He even massaged Aldo's feet to help relieve the muscle contractions in them. I once asked him if it wasn't difficult to see Aldo like this. He answered that Aldo was still the same old Aldo, only better.

God bless Bradley!

A teacher from Aldo's previous school brought his classmates from 2005 and 2006 to visit him at the end of each year. It meant a lot to me, but he'd become a stranger to them and they kept their distance form him. After such a visit, Aldo sat on the porch, staring out across the dam. He hid his face and made his crying sound. When I asked him what the matter was, he just asked me to pray with him. He wrote about it in his journal the next day. Although he was reaching out to them, he knew that they belonged to a time that had passed forever. They didn't come back either. I guess because they didn't know how to react to him. They'd gone on with their lives and he had remained behind.

We took Aldo to the crowning ceremony of the Miss South Africa Pageant, because we knew he would enjoy it. By then, he could write and talk and spiritually he'd grown tremendously. A woman and a little girl walked by just as Aldo spoke to us. When Aldo speaks, he lifts up his hand. We don't know why he does it, and we're trying to teach him *not* to do it, but this girl saw it. "Look at that child! What a freak!" she exclaimed. Tinus and I just looked at each other. I was distressed to see that Aldo had heard what she'd said. He immediately told me to forgive her, but I was too overcome by emotion. I excused myself, went back to the hotel room and cried like my heart was breaking. I told God that I didn't think I could go on any further. People can be so cruel.

Another such incident happened when a precious friend brought something over to the house for me. Her children remained in the car when she came to the porch. I asked her why they weren't coming in and she answered that they were uncomfortable with Aldo. Aldo, who was standing within earshot, turned around and started walking towards the house. He fell down on the stairs, but kept going, eventually crawling up the stairs and into the house. He went into his room and closed the door.

My heart was breaking. I looked at the woman and knew I had to forgive her, since I too needed God's forgiveness in my life.

Few people came to visit us during that time, and those who did come, came without their children.

> I really want to play with my friends again. I just want to live like other people.

We've found that children in general don't know how to react to a disabled person, and would rather steer clear than reach out to him. I started wishing that people would rather not come to see us at all, than for them to come without their children. To me it felt like they thought that Aldo wasn't good enough to communicate with their children. I know that Aldo was also hurt by this and I blamed the parents. Many friendships were weighed and found wanting.

Our support system had failed us and I learnt that I cannot rely on other people. We had to hold fast to our faith and rely on God alone. Today I can say that God has helped me to forgive everyone who'd hurt us whether deliberately or unwittingly. I'm even grateful that God has led us down this path. I know that I can only reach the destination if I'm willing to die to myself and with Christ so that I can *live* with Him too.

It's been three years since the accident. Aldo's health and physical well-being improve every day. He and Patrys attend a private school where they've

accepted him and showed us much love. He even plays soccer with the other children. He wears a helmet and kneepads, because he falls down a lot. He runs four paces and falls four paces. He always gets back up to run and stumble some more. There seem to be bumps on his head all the time and his legs and knees are constantly skinned.

In April 2006 Aldo wrote:

> I will play soccer again one day. Please, Mommy, will you help me with my walking and with my speaking. I know I will run again and preach the Gospel. God will send us all over the world and we will tell everyone that Jesus is alive!

Many times the children at his school will grab him by the arms and run with him across the soccer field. I cannot tell you what it means to me! I will never be able to express my gratitude to each of those children who love him, and have accepted him so unconditionally.

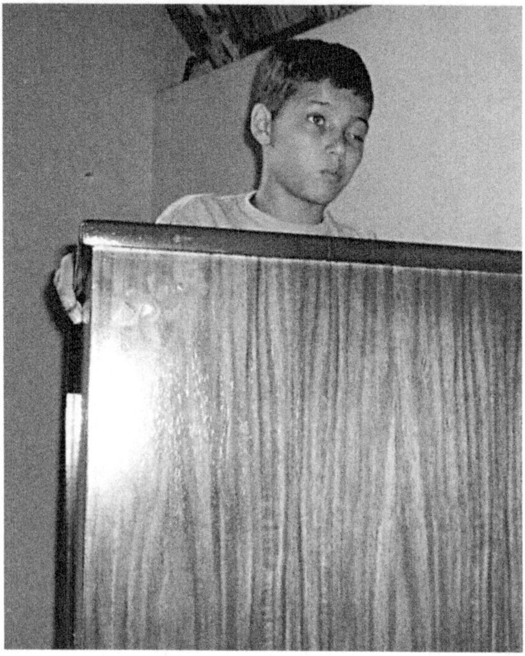

EXPECTING THE BRIDEGROOM

In the evenings when Aldo and Josh bath together, Aldo will sometimes call loudly: "Jesus! Jesus!" Following his big brother's lead, Josh will do the same. They make such racket that I have to close the windows and doors for fear of what the neighbours might think. "Aldo, why do you call out for Jesus when you're in the bath?" I asked him one night while sitting on the edge.

"I want Jesus to come and get me, because it's so much better in heaven than here on Earth," he answered. He told me once that his house in heaven already has his name on it. "Mommy, you have to pray with me that Jesus will come and take me to heaven," he said.

Oh my darling boy, if only you knew how much I'd prayed to keep you here a while longer!

Someone recently told Aldo that he is afraid of dying. The very next day, Aldo wrote this to everyone who is seeking God's face:

> To everyone who seeks the presence of Jesus like me,
> Be prepared for when He comes back for us. It will happen sooner than we think. Won't you please accept Him as your personal Saviour? If you don't, you will go to hell. Please do it soon while you still have the chance to do it. Jesus has already paid the complete price for you and me. He showed me everything in heaven and in hell. Believe me when I say, you don't want to go to hell. Please, won't you accept Jesus right now? Jesus loves you so much, believe me. You are the reason why He sent me back. I didn't want to come back, but He sent me back so that you can be ready for His return.

Aldo often talks about the golden bridge at the gates of heaven. One day he hid his head in his arms and made the crying sound. I asked him why he was crying.

"There is a huge golden bridge (in heaven). Many thousands of people are streaming across the bridge to get to the gate of pearls on the other side. But when they get there they can't get in. They just stand at the gate and cry," he explained.

"Why can't they go in, Aldo?"

"Don't you know, Mommy? There is a wedding going on inside, but the people outside are wearing clothes of mud and that's why they can't go in. They weren't ready."

"Clothes of mud?"

"Yes, they're all muddy, because they don't know Jesus."

Jesus didn't come to this earth so that we may have a religion! He gave His life so that we may have an intimate love relationship with God.

The day after Aldo and I spoke about the golden bridge in heaven, he wrote down only two words: Matthew 25. I went and read the entire chapter in my Bible. It's about the 10 young virgins. They represent the churchgoers; those who call themselves Christians. All ten of them had oil in their lamps and expected the bridegroom, but only five were really prepared for his return. The bride of God has to be ready for when He returns. You cannot wait until you see Him coming, before you ready yourself. You have to do it now! The trumpets are already sounding, and still the bride isn't ready.

When I read this, I fell to my knees and prayed. I told God that I would stay on my knees until He showed me how to get to the place where He wanted me to be. I wanted to be ready for His return. I wasn't going to walk this uphill road on Earth, only to discover that I wasn't ready when He returned. Like Jacob, I was clinging to God and I was determined to hold on, until He blessed me.

I waited on God. Often we give up too quickly in prayer. Instead, we should persevere in prayer until we enter into His presence so that we may receive a Rhema-word (a living word) that will change our lives. While praying that day, I had such a breakthrough. I realized at once that I was like an egg, hidden inside a beautiful shell that I was constantly polishing. It is a selfish way of living, because everything in your life is about you. I lived like that before I met Jesus: I was in control of my life and everything centered on me. It was my way, or the high way.

The problem is that the nourishing part of an egg is on the inside. The shell has to break before the nutritious egg can be used to feed someone. I had to die to myself (my shell had to break) before I could become one with God, just like one would mix egg and flour together to bake bread.

Experience has also taught me that you cannot choose who or how the mixing will be done. There have been days when I cried to God in anguish; times when I couldn't understand why this tragedy had to befall *my* child. "Why, Lord? Why?" I would ask. I want answers! But that's just it. Faith doesn't need answers. Faith is sure of the things we hope for; *"and certain of what we do not see,"* (Heb. 11:1). Faith accepts that God knows the answers.

The mixing process is different for everyone, depending on your specific circumstances. But this I know for sure: we are on Earth for one reason, and that is to glorify God. The more time we spend with God, the more He can shape our character to resemble Him. And so the egg and the Flour are mixed until it becomes impossible to separate these two again. When I realized this, Rom. 8:35-39 became Rhema to me. I knew then that *nothing* would ever separate me from the love of God and that's why I can claim the promise in Jh. 14:13-14 that whatever I may ask in His name, I shall receive it.

The egg and Flour mixture is then placed in a pan and baked in a hot oven. The oven of my life was so hot sometimes, that I wanted to flee, but I couldn't. God's character was being formed in me. I shared this simile with Tinus once and remarked that people, who weren't in God's inferno, still did exactly what they pleased. "That's why we should pray for them," he answered, "for there is no better place than where we are now."

When the bread is finally lifted out of the pan, it's placed on a plate. The Host breaks it and its aroma spreads throughout the house. I can almost hear God saying, "Only now can I feed the world with you. Now we are one and you know that *nothing* can separate you from Me again."

Shortly after I had this epiphany, Aldo started writing about the bride in his journal. He writes that Jesus is coming back for His bride, and he often encourages me to tell the world about it.

God has been speaking to me about the bride as well, and specifically about how she will behave in His presence. The bride will have an intimate and loving relationship with the Groom. They will commune as Husband and wife, because she will be an adult. The bride isn't forced into this most intimate relationship. She chose it when she surrendered her life to Him and because of this surrender she will be clothed in His glory.

The bride has to be a mature adult, because God won't share His secrets with an immature youth. He reveals everything to His bride as she lies peacefully on His chest, listening not only to His voice, but also to His very heartbeat.

God's Word is a living Word. Jesus has gone to prepare a place for His bride in heaven. You and I are the bride. Will you say "Yes!" to the Bridegroom? Together we will dance and sing. Give Him your life and become the bride. Because we have God's Spirit, we can live a holy life. I am His bride; what about you?

While the bride is still here on Earth, she serves all God's children. Even when she's tired, she keeps working for Him. Although she doesn't know exactly when He will arrive, she is always expecting Him. She is constantly changing, growing and maturing. Every time she enters into His presence, she becomes more like Him. He is reflected in her eyes and when He looks at her, He sees only the blood of Jesus that covers her. When she goes out into the world and they look at her, they see God. The Spirit of God also dwells in His bride and in this way they are already one.

JESUS IS COMING FOR HIS BRIDE!

Jesus has gone to prepare a dwelling place for His bride in heaven, but not all Christians will be part of the bride. Only those who chose to lay down their lives will go in to the wedding feast. Will you say "Yes!" to the bridegroom? He is waiting for you to give up control of your life and become His bride. Although everyone was invited to the wedding, each person has to make their own decision to give up their lives in order to become the bride.

> He wants to come and fetch His bride, but she is not ready. She must stop sinning because God's bride is holy. Mommy, you must tell everyone that we are the Laodicea church. God will judge those who don't accept Him.

The psalmist asks in Ps. 15:1: *"Lord, whom may dwell in your sanctuary? Who may live on your holy hill?"* And then God answers in verse 2; *"He whose walk is blameless and who does what is righteous..."* These are high criteria – to be blameless and righteous. But through the blood of Jesus, we've been sanctified and thus we can enter through the salvation of God in Jesus Christ.

If God is speaking to you now, obey Him. Lay down your life and become part of the bride today!

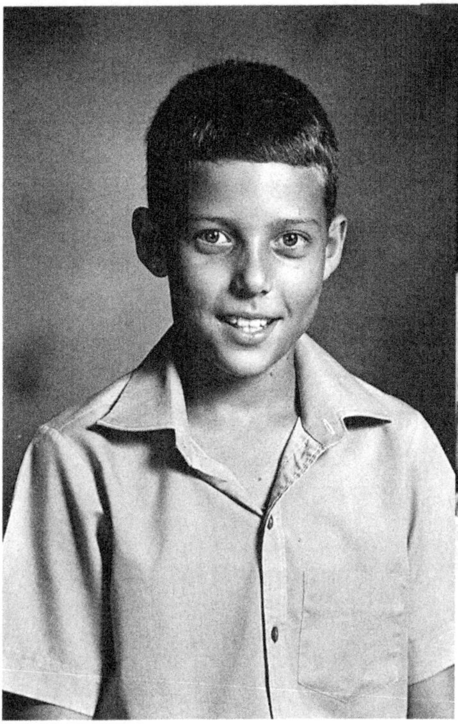

A NEW REALITY

It took me a long time before I could muster up the courage to write this chapter. I would like nothing better than to tell you that Aldo has recovered 100%; that he is just as healthy as he was before, but I can't. The road to recovery for people with head injuries is a long and exhausting one. Still, when I think about all the negative prognoses he's received, his recovery to date is nothing short of miraculous. Aldo can walk, although it is slow going and because he still has trouble with balance and he falls down a lot. He gets tired easily and then becomes emotional and difficult. I suppose in that he's just like every other teenager.

Aldo still cannot laugh out loud, but the soft smile around the corners of his mouth brings tears to my eyes.

The injury to his mid-brain still makes it difficult for him to sleep and he often comes crawling into our bed between 3:00 and 4:00 in the mornings. I smile in the dark as I make space for him. When I feel his long legs curling around me, I thank God that he is alive and here with us. Then those long awkward arms embrace me and he says, "I love you, Mommy," and all is right with the world.

On the road to recovery, some days are better than others. Aldo's right hand still goes up in the air involuntarily every time he speaks. We are trying to teach him to keep that hand in his pocket when he is around people, but it doesn't always work. He came home one day with the thumb on his right hand painfully swollen. He didn't want to talk about it, but after a while the story emerged. His hand had lifted again when he was speaking and a classmate of his nearly broke his finger. The boy explained that he did it because it "irritated" him when Aldo's hand goes up like that every time.

"What do I say to this, Lord?" I prayed silently. "How much more can we endure?"

All I could do was to hug Aldo tightly to me, get some salve and bandage the thumb. It's like I said: Some days are worse than others.

Aldo's one eyelid still droops, but I'm not giving up on any aspect of his recovery. I speak life and trust that God will heal that nerve too.

Aldo speaks slowly and in monotone, but at least he speaks clearly. However, not everyone has the time or patience to listen to him. I have seen the pain in his eyes when people walk off while he's in mid-sentence, or even shuts him up because they are in a hurry. In moments like these I feel like crying. How many times before the accident did I too tell him to be quiet? And then I remember the months of silence that followed when I was constantly praying that God should have mercy on me. "Just let him speak again, Lord!" I pleaded. That's why I always listen patiently to my precious boy no matter how rushed I am.

Aldo is a teenager and like other teenage boys of his age, he notices pretty girls.

"Why don't they notice me, Mom?" he asked me more than once. "Is it because of my eye or the way that I talk?"

It breaks my heart. All I have are the promises in God's Word. I tell my son, "Jesus has a plan for your life, a bright future and an amazing wife. She will adore you and the two of you will travel the world testifying and proclaiming the Word of God. Believe me, Aldo. I know God has already predestined a very special woman for you. She'll be your right hand, because yours shakes and moves at random. She will love you unconditionally and she will love God and belong to Him. She will love you despite your disability and she will accept you completely because her spirit will be one with God's Spirit."

My son is a lot quieter than he used to be. Even when he is surrounded by many people, he will close his eyes and pray. He prays constantly and I know he is building a spiritual house of prayer. Many nights I find him on his knees, waiting on God. I also know that Aldo has the gift of prophesy and many times he will quote Scripture that I don't even know myself. When I ask him how he knows about it, his answer is always the same:

"Jesus wrote the Word on my heart when I was in heaven with Him. I was dead, but God came and blew His Holy Spirit into me, and I was alive!"

Jesus says I have to accept the fact that I'm back on Earth. I accept it now, and I wil get better. Please keep believing that it will happen and you will see my healing with your own eyes. Thank you for loving me. Thank you for loving Jesus too. Together we will proclaim God's Word because He has chosen us for the end time. Mommy has to keep speaking, until I can do it.

Aldo is improving on a daily basis. On April 30, 2007, he turned 15. He and Tinus have taken to cycling and have entered a few cycle races in the tandem category, since Aldo's balance isn't quite perfect yet. He also regularly goes horse riding and exercises at the sport rehabilitation centre at Pretoria University. They are also teaching him to walk properly. When he finally gets home after all his activities in the afternoon, he is utterly exhausted, but he is making progress. He walks much better now and can climb stairs. He can even remove the tarpaulin on the pool and he enjoys swimming. I often watch from my office window as he plays and splashes about in the water. In moments like these, I'm just so grateful to God for His mercy. My mosaic is finally taking on a new form. It is coming into focus. Although I still don't know what the future will bring for Aldo, I believe that God will finish the work He has started in my son. But whether I live to see it or not, I will serve God with my all and everything. I have great hope, in a great God who cares so much that He gave His only Son, so that Tinus and Josh, and Aldo and I could live!

CALLED TO TESTIFY

I've always wanted a closer walk with God and to share in the abundance of the life He promises. I hungered for Him; desired Him to be my First and my Last; my breath, yes the very blood in my veins. I wanted Him to be *in* me and I wanted to be *in* Him.

But the road we were travelling was not an easy one, and we cried out to God for help. "Lord," I said, "I know I'm a new creation now. Your Spirit and mine are the same, but please Holy Spirit, teach me to walk in the way of righteousness."

One day, when I was cleaning Aldo's trachea, God told me to go back to the Word. "My Word is full of truths. Use them to find a life of abundance. I give you these truths as a gift. Don't view them as laws, since My blood has already freed you from the law. Rather see them as route markers on your journey with Me. Allow My Spirit to work through you. Stop all your clever arguments; your logical disputes. Faith starts where logic ends. And then miracles follow."

An expectation started building within me. I expected to find in God what I was unable to find anywhere else. I realized that I was nothing without God.

So, I opened my heart and tried to listen closely whenever God spoke. Over a period of time the Holy Spirit has given me principles to live by that I would like to share with you in the second part of this book.

After I had tried everything, I finally discovered the secret to living life in abundance: It is only found in a love relationship with the King of all kings.

We can only live a victorious life, if we remain in His presence every minute of the day. The only way we can be constantly aware of His Holy presence, is to pray continuously. I don't know why we find this so difficult to do. When you love someone, you want to be with that person and you want to talk him/her constantly. Nothing could give you more joy than to share your whole life with your beloved! You just want to enjoy each other and give to one another. Why is it so hard for us to view our relationship with God in this way?

Perhaps it's because our own marriages are often lacking. There are countless books on marriage, but all that knowledge and insight will come to naught if you don't love your spouse unconditionally; if you're not willing to lay down your life for your partner. If you want a fulfilled relationship in your marriage, you have to die unto yourself and surrender your life to your beloved.

This is what God did for us. Think about it. He loved us first and He gave His life for us. *"Greater love has no one than this that he lay down his life for his friends."* – Jn. 15:13. He was despised and deserted by people (and by the Father), but He endured it for our sakes. By His blood we were saved and through His stripes we are healed!

When I understood the significance of the blood of Jesus, my entire life changed. I was set free from the expectations and limitations of the world.

> I WAS SET FREE BY THE BLOOD OF THE LAMB.

I plead the blood of Jesus over my family on a daily basis. I also pray for a wall of fire to protect us from every evil force and power that may come against us. It is not a ritual to me, but a natural part of my love relationship with God through the blood covenant with Jesus. In doing this, I claim all the advantages of Christ's death on the cross for me. Whenever I see the hand of the enemy in a situation, I proclaim the blood of Jesus, saying, "Satan, you have no authority here. The blood of Jesus opposes you!"

It is unfortunate that so few ministers preach on the topic of the blood of Jesus, because few Christians understand the power of it. Demons recognize the power of His blood and they flee before it and Satan is defenceless against it. If only we knew more about the blood of the Lamb and were able to use it more! When you ask God to cover you with His blood, you acknowledge and honor Him and the Name that is above all names: Jesus Christ.

"Share your knowledge of My blood with My children," said the Holy Spirit. "For they don't understand it."

I repeat: The blood of Jesus sets you free!

I also ask God to fill me with the Holy Spirit every day. It doesn't mean that I'm reborn every day, but I give myself to Him, body, mind and soul, every day.

"Fill me with new oil, Lord. I want new oil, because old oil has a foul smell." Have you seen all the heavy pieces of dirt that settles at the bottom of old, used oil? Old oil will not do. You need a new, fresh anointing every day. You have to gather your manna every morning.

I rejoice in every circumstance in my life, whether good or bad because no matter what happens, I know that He is my Alpha and Omega, my Beginning and my End. This is reason enough to celebrate.

Prayer has become a large part of my life. I know that He answers our prayers because of the blood of Jesus that has cleansed us from all sin and gave us free passage to the throne of grace.

My desire is to spend as much time as possible in His presence and to draw ever closer to the Him, to experience His purifying fire so that His light might reflect through me. Yes, I want to reflect God to the world. Who are you reflecting?

Living in God's presence, I have come to know the fire that surrounds Him. This purifying fire destroyed every tie that bound me to the world or my selfish desires. I was saved like one plucked from the fire (Zech. 3:2). God is a kind God who saves us from ourselves.

No one can force you into a relationship with anyone. God is a gentleman. He won't force Himself on you. You have to *choose* if you want to have a love relationship with Him. Only when you accept Him and receive Him, can you be truly happy. Our happiness isn't centred in ourselves or in our circumstances, or even in our relationship with people.

Our happiness lies in our unity with God.

No person can make you happy or fulfill your needs. You need to drink from the fountain of living water to be truly satisfied. Jn. 4:14: *"but whoever drinks the water I give him will never thirst. Indeed, the water I give him will become in him a spring of water welling up to eternal life."* You can never hope to feed and satisfy the spiritual man with worldly food or treasures. True happiness can only be found in our love relationship with God. The more I fed my spirit on God's Word, the more I wanted to praise and worship Him.

God has opened my eyes. I see His Word as a lighthouse; a beacon in every dark situation. I started feeding my spirit with the Word of God, and with the guidance of the Holy Spirit, I found the principles to an abundant life. God's holy Fire started burning in me and gave me light. The closer I drew to Him, the brighter it shone. And the darkness fled before His light.

What follows in the next section of the book is what I've learnt through the Holy Spirit regarding how to attain the life of abundance that God intended for us. These are not absolute rules or doctrine, but principles or keys to living a spirit-filled life with Jesus. But there is a price to be paid for abundance. For me, it boils down to this: I approach God's throne of grace through the blood of Jesus that sanctifies me. I give myself to Him as I lay down my life before the King of kings. And then I just bask in His love.

The things I will suggest to you in the next part of this book have become route markers to me on my journey to abundance.

PART 2

DISCOVER AN ABUNDANT LIFE

Jy sal ons self met die
Hy en krag saam se
ons God se woord verkondig
mamma moet mense
vertel dat Jesus lewe
ek het Hom gesien saam
met Moses en Abraham
God het op Sy troon gesit
en Hy het vir my gese
dat ek moet vir die mense
vertel dat daar 'n hemel
en 'n hel is. Daarom het
Hy my terug gestuur, gaan
en vertel asb tot ek dit self
kan doen

*All Afrikaans letters are Aldo's original letters - see translation of these on opposite pages.

MONDAY, OCTOBER 24, 2005

YOU WILL ANOINT US WITH OIL. THE HOLY SPIRIT WILL GUIDE US AND GIVE US POWER TO PREACH GOD'S WORD. MOMMY, YOU HAVE TO TELL PEOPLE THAT JESUS LIVES! I SAW HIM AND MOSES AND ABRAHAM. GOD WAS SITTING ON HIS THRONE AND HE TOLD ME TO TELL PEOPLE THAT THERE IS A HEAVEN AND A HELL. THAT'S WHY HE SENT ME BACK. PLEASE GO AND TELL EVERYONE ABOUT THIS, UNTIL I CAN DO IT MYSELF. WHEN I'M 16-YEARS-OLD, I WILL PREACH GOD'S WORD MYSELF. WILL WE GO FEARLESSLY WHEREVER HE SENDS US? HE WILL ANOINT YOUR TONGUE SO THAT YOU WILL SPEAK ENGLISH WHEN YOU TESTIFY OVERSEAS.

> JOB 3:25: WHAT I FEARED HAS COME UPON ME; WHAT I DREADED HAS HAPPENED TO ME.

The first principle to living a spirit-filled life is to acknowledge and defeat fear. Remember fear opposes love as evil opposes Good.

I'm ashamed to admit it, but all my life I feared that my family and I would be involved in a car accident. My biggest fear was that something would happen to either my husband or my children. I really dreaded it.

Tell me what you fear, and I'll tell you what will happen to you.

One way of defeating your fear is found in 2 Cor. 10:5: *"We demolish arguments and every pretension that sets itself up against the knowledge of God, and we take captive every thought to make it obedient to Christ."*

In order to overcome your fear, you have to fight every negative thought tooth and nail, because these thoughts are from your enemy who wants to steal your faith and joy. Align your thoughts with God's will in every situation. For example, when you are waiting for the results of blood tests, don't allow fear to take control of your thoughts. Instead remind yourself that disease isn't God's will for us. Read Scripture that affirms this and think positively. Don't allow even one "what if?" Fear opens the door for Satan to attack us, because fear destroys faith. Don't give in to negative or destructive thoughts. Control your thoughts or they will control you!

After the accident, our fear was largely due to our ignorance regarding Aldo's injuries and moreover it was a natural human response to the trauma that we had suffered. God's reaction however, was to sow faith and hope in our hearts. We've since learnt to think healthy thoughts about Aldo's life and future.

> Mommy, will you please keep believing and not give up? Keep believing and don't be afraid.

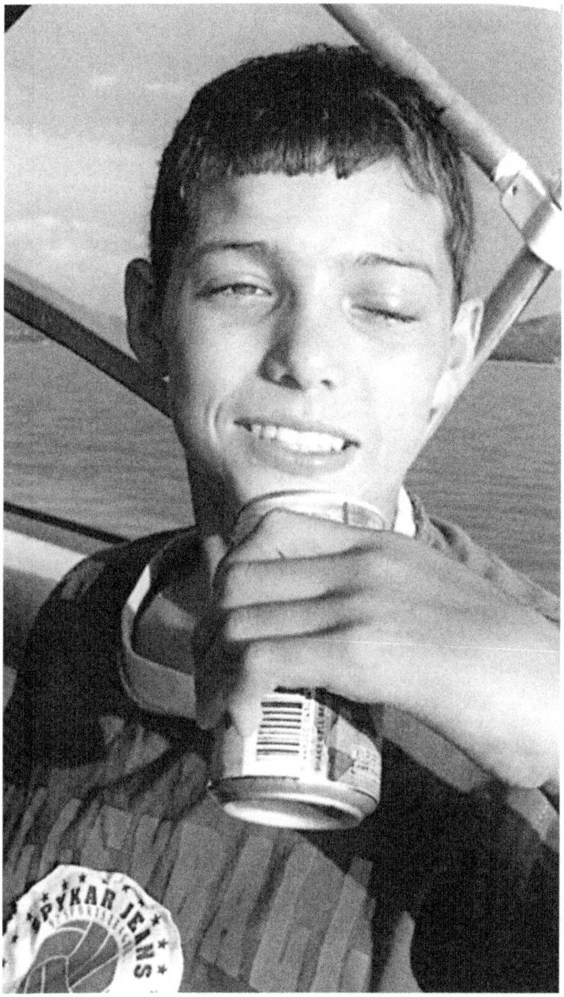

God's children will seek His Spirit. God will heal me.

Ongelukke gebeur maar want ons
is op die aarde. God sal on
nie begewe of verlaat nie. God
sal my gesond maak en ek
gaan Sy woord verkondig.

WEDNESDAY, FEBRUARY 1, 2006

ACCIDENTS HAPPEN BECAUSE WE ARE ON EARTH. GOD WILL NOT LEAVE US OR FORSAKE US. GOD WILL HEAL ME AND I SHALL PREACH HIS WORD. I WILL LEAD THOSE WHO ARE LOST OUT OF THEIR DESPAIR UNDER THE CLOUD, JUST LIKE MOSES DID. PLEASE, WILL YOU ANOINT AND BLESS ME? WE WILL DECLARE GOD'S WORD TOGETHER.

LK. 9:62: JESUS REPLIED, 'NO ONE WHO PUTS HIS HAND TO THE PLOW AND LOOKS BACK IS FIT FOR SERVICE IN THE KINGDOM OF GOD'.

As an image consultant, I know how important appearance is. I know all about changing your image.

Often when I was by myself, I would sit with a picture of Aldo before the accident in my one hand, and a picture of him after the accident in the other. Looking at these before and after shots, I would cry inconsolably. Until one day when the Holy Spirit asked, "Retha, what are you doing?"

"I suppose I'm feeling sorry for myself, Father. I had so many dreams for him."

"Don't you realize that he is no longer your son? You sacrificed him to me, remember? He belongs to me now. His life is in My hands. Do you remember what happened to Lot's wife when she looked back?"

"Yes, she became a salt pillar, Lord."

"Whenever she looked back, she had a change of heart, doubting the wisdom of leaving behind her earthly possessions. When an athlete runs in a race, she doesn't look back for fear of losing her focus and falling, which will also endanger the other athletes."

I suddenly thought of the time when Peter walked on the sea towards Jesus. Instantly I got it: Peter was doing fine while he kept his eyes on Jesus, but the minute he started focusing on external circumstances like the storm and waves (the world around him), he started to sink.

"Don't look back, Retha. In this race you have to keep your eyes fixed on Me. I know you can hear the crowd screaming that you have to face reality, but I want you to think about Jairus.

"When Jairus heard that his daughter had died, he was just as frightened as you are now. But he turned to Me and looked into My eyes. I told him then as I'm telling you now, 'Don't be alarmed. Have faith in Me!' Retha, I *am* in control!"

We all have a history. I don't know what your past looks like. Perhaps you are trying to recapture the past when you were young and idealistic, hoping to relive happier times. Or, maybe you are desperate to undo the mistakes you might have made early on in your life. No matter what your reasons are for wanting to revive the past, you can't do it. The past is dead and gone. You can't change a thing about it or bring it into the present.

You also cannot do anything about the future. It is in God's hands. All you can work with is the here and the now. Deal with your present reality without looking over your shoulder. Ask God what He wants you to do *today* and leave the past behind. Look to the future instead.

We don't have to see the road ahead of us to take the first step in faith. God will make the way. God sees the entire road. He has the map. In Gen. 22:8, He showed me His vision for Aldo and it has kept me going till now. It reads: *"... God himself will provide the lamb for the burnt offering, my son. And the two of them went on together."*

Don't look back. God has the burnt offering ready!

23 Jan

Jy moet met pappa vrede maak
Jesus wil he jy moet pappa lief he
saas jy Hom het
Jesus se pappa kry baie swaar
ons moet hom baie lief hê ons
moet ons beste vir hom gee.
Ek is lief vir pappa met
my hele hart siel
en verstand
Jesus gaan pappa seën
vir wat hy alles doen
vir ons.!
mamma moet my help om
om pappa gelukkig te maak Hy is
baie ongelukkig ons gaan hom
verloor so Liefde is al wat
pappa vra hy moet hom liefde gee

Jesus praat met my ons moet
luister as Hy praat
en Hy is lief vir ons gesin
pappa wil vir jou soen
vandag

Monday, January 23, 2005

You have to make peace with Daddy. Jesus wants it. He wants you to love Daddy like He loves him. Jesus says that Daddy is suffering and we have to give him our love. We have to give ourselves to Him. I love Daddy with my whole heart, soul and mind. Jesus will bless Daddy for everything the does for me. Mommy, you have to help me to make Daddy happy, or we could lose him. Daddy only needs love. Mommy, you have to love Daddy. Jesus is speaking to us about this and we must obey Him. He loves our family. Today, Daddy wants to kiss you, Mommy.

> Eph. 4:26, In your anger, do not sin: Do not let the sun go down while you are still angry, and do not give the devil a foothold.

Are you walking in the power of forgiveness or are you wallowing in bitterness?

Forgiveness removes the sting of sin. When you forgive, the venom in the serpent's bite is neutralized. You are effectively stopping the poison in your blood and thereby foiling death. Although God gives you the strength to do it, only you can make the choice to forgive.

I struggled with forgiveness after the accident. If someone were to ask me if I blamed Tinus for what had happened, I would immediately say that I knew it wasn't his fault. But still deep down inside me, I was furious with him. I guess I had to blame *someone* for what happened in order to remain sane!

Our marriage suffered a lot in that time. I kept up appearances, but the poison of bitterness and resentment took its toll. I became physically ill with the effects of bitterness. I kept losing weight, literally shrinking as the bitterness kept gnawing away at me.

Then Aldo wrote:

> Mommy, you have to forgive Daddy. It wasn't his fault! Jesus wants you to do it right now. He cannot use you while you're filled with such bitterness!

I was taken aback. Except for God, nobody knew that I really blamed Tinus in my heart of hearts. I had to decide whether I would allow God's Word to control me, or whether I would let my self-centered emotions rule my life. I chose God's Word and acquitted Tinus.

My setting Tinus free like that marks the beginning of God's work in him too. Tinus and I became one again. Our unity has been restored and since then Tinus has also experienced a closer walk with God. Tinus needed my forgiveness in order to forgive himself and move on. I honor God for using Aldo, even before he could speak, to tell me to forgive his father.

Anger and bitterness almost cost me dearly, but I learnt a valuable lesson in the process: the enemy will use our refusal to forgive to steal our joy and peace. Forgiving people comes easier for me nowadays. I make a deliberate effort to forgive people when they hurt me. Then I may receive God's peace and go on with my life. It is what God expects from His children. He says in Heb. 12:14, *"Make every effort to live in peace with all men and to be holy, without holiness no one will see the Lord".*

Another testimony that emphasises the importance of forgiveness is that of the Nigerian pastor of whom the prophetess had told me in hospital. He appears in a film called "The Lazarus Phenomenon" that tells the stories of people who had also experienced heaven like Aldo did. In this film, the pastor testifies that he was dead for four days before God resurrected him. During this time, he too was in heaven. However, because his heart was unforgiving, he would have ended up in hell, he says, if God hadn't given him a second chance.

When I heard this, I thought, "Lord, how can this be? The man is a pastor!"

"That doesn't matter," came the reply. "I'm not interested in the works of man. No one who harbors bitterness in his heart will enter into the kingdom of God, because God is love."

Only the love of God can loosen the roots of bitterness in your heart. And without the indwelling of the Holy Spirit we won't be able to forgive anyone. We cannot afford others what we don't possess ourselves! It's only after you've received Jesus' forgiveness that you can forgive someone else.

Forgiveness starts in a heart that is willing to leave the past behind.

Many marriages are nothing more than an endless fight. Like an unending boxing match each day brings a new round of arguing and hostility. Over time husbands and wives become so used to the anger that it becomes the only way they communicate. After years of bickering and biting I doubt if they can even remember what they're so angry about. Put those hurts in perspective: your husband or wife is only human after all. Then forgive each other before it is too late.

When I say this, people often ask me if it means they're not allowed to get divorced. The fact of the matter is, I don't know where your journey with God may lead you, but whether you get divorced or decide to stick it out, you will have to forgive!

Forgiving someone isn't easy and our feelings of anger and resentment may not disappear over night. Take heart though: the blood of Jesus will be like salve on your wound and in time, the Holy Spirit will heal it from the inside out. Even if you can still feel it throbbing in the beginning, don't take a needle and gash it open again. In time the pain will lessen and you'll become aware of God's healing power.

Don't allow pain and anger to fester in your heart. Ask God's forgiveness for your own iniquities and forgive others as you want Him to forgive you. If you do this, you will bask in His peace.

CENTURION
VELO

Jesus se ons moet begin dankie se vir die ongeluk want nou eers kan God met ons lewe doen wat Hy beplan het. Mamma jou lewe behoort aan Jesus. Ek sien die troonkamer en Jesus se Hy sal ons kom haal ons moet net geduldig wees. Ons gaan ons self offer aan God.

WEDNESDAY, OCTOBER 26, 2005

JESUS SAYS WE HAVE TO BE GRATEFUL FOR THE ACCIDENT, BECAUSE ONLY NOW CAN GOD ACCOMPLISH WHAT HE HAD PLANNED FOR US. MOMMY, YOUR LIFE BELONGS TO JESUS. I SEE THE THRONE ROOM AND JESUS IS SAYING HE WILL COME TO GET US. WE JUST HAVE TO BE PATIENT. WE WILL SACRIFICE OURSELVES TO GOD.

1 THES. 5:16-18: BE JOYFUL ALWAYS; PRAY CONTINUALLY; GIVE THANKS IN ALL CIRCUMSTANCES, FOR THIS IS GOD'S WILL FOR YOU IN CHRIST JESUS.

Please bear in mind that I'm no theologian. I'm just Retha. That which I know about God, is what He teaches me through the Spirit. One such lesson is on thanksgiving. The Spirit says, "Retha, I want you to rejoice about everything that I've allowed to happen in you life. You have to praise Me. Rejoice and sing about everything in your life."

After all, why should God add *anything* to my life, if I don't even appreciate what I have right now?

The bumps on Aldo's head are ever increasing. The bruises don't heal either, since he keeps hitting his head in the same places. He falls down at school, then comes home and, in an attempt to kick a soccer ball, he loses his balance and falls right through a large window, cutting himself in the process. The very next day, he stumbles over Josh's toy car and, because he's too slow to brace himself, falls directly on his head. He bleeds profusely. Josh applies pressure and I drive like a maniac to get him stitched up. It's only after the boys are finally off to school, that I can sit down and try to gather my thoughts. Then I start crying.

"Lord, things are not getting any better. It's too hard, Lord. The suffering is too much to bear," I sob.

"Retha, I want you to rejoice and praise Me in all your circumstances."

"It's so hard, Lord. You'll have to help me with this."

Since I've started to rejoice and praise God in all my circumstances, I have come to understand what Paul means when he says that he will only boast in those things that show his weaknesses (2 Cor. 11:30) because then the power of God can act in and through me.

Our family truly believes that God is in control of absolutely everything in our lives. Of course God knew about the accident even before it happened, just like He knew that Peter would betray Him before the crucifixion. I don't believe the accident was His will, but He allowed it to happen just like He allowed Satan to test Job. God sees farther than we do. He saw the joy and victory of the resurrection, when His disciples could only see His death, and He knew that Job's suffering would ultimately glorify His name.

I'm constantly reminded of what God said to me in the throne room: "Your life on Earth is not about you, Retha. It's all about Me." So despite my circumstances and my inability to restore things, I praise God for *everything* in my life now. He keeps me on my knees and humble.

When you pray, don't moan and groan and demand. Instead, turn your prayer time into a praise and worship celebration!

God showed Samuel His heart's desires. Become more like Samuel by setting yourself apart for God. Together we'll go into God's secret place.

Wees soos Jesus jou wil hê

heilig. God wil jou heilig hê

vir Hom. Soos ons geheilig is

deur Sy bloed

God gaan ons seën ek

sal gesond word en ek sal

ook Sy woord verkondig.

God sal ons self leer en

dan sal ons mense leer.

Sal ja my altyd so liefhe

Ons sal altyd saam werk

en mense bedien.

SUNDAY, NOVEMBER 27, 2005

BE HOLY. GOD WANTS YOU TO BE HOLY FOR HIM. WE WERE MADE HOLY BY THE BLOOD OF JESUS. GOD WILL BLESS US AND I WILL BE HEALED. I WILL ALSO PROCLAIM HIS WORD. GOD WILL TEACH US HIMSELF AND THEN WE WILL TEACH OTHER PEOPLE. WILL YOU ALWAYS LOVE ME MOMMY? WE WILL ALWAYS WORK TOGETHER AND SERVE HIS PEOPLE.

> ROM. 8:28: AND WE KNOW THAT IN ALL THINGS GOD WORKS FOR THE GOOD OF THOSE WHO LOVE HIM, WHO HAVE BEEN CALLED ACCORDING TO HIS PURPOSE.

Our God is able to turn every situation around to His honor so that He may accomplish His good works through our lives. He even takes our mistakes and changes them into miracles if we trust Him completely. Then our suffering will become His mercy. Our embarrassments are His opportunities to show us His favor and grace.

There are times, though, when God may ask you to step out in faith so that you may see for yourself that He will make everything work to your advantage. Taking this first step in faith often means stepping out of your comfort zone, and it can be daunting. But moving out of this secure space is a good thing since no growth can take place when you are that much at ease. In fact, staying in your comfort zone may very well keep you from fulfilling God's perfect plan in and with your life.

The day I finally declared that I could go no further, I discovered the treasure that is mentioned in Mt. 13:44: *"The kingdom of heaven is like treasure hidden in a field. When a man found it, he hid it again, and then in his joy went and sold all he had and bought that field."*

Retha, the new creation, had finally seen the Light. My body was simply the vehicle through which God would accomplish all the good deeds He had planned for me. I have learnt to stay in the palm of His hand even in those times when I felt that I too was walking on water. I had to abandon all the trust I had in myself, my own abilities, talents and skills. I had to trust God completely and I had to be willing to obey Him at all cost.

When you obey God like that, He will often ask you to step out of your comfort zone. He wants you to attain higher heights; to grow spiritually. Every time He calls you, you will have to lay down your own will. But when you move out in faith like this, you are acknowledging His sovereign will and it will deepen your relationship with Him. As you do this your dependence on Him will increase too and His power will propel you forward. In time, there will be less and less of you, and more and more of Him.

The task God has given our family sometimes overwhelms me. It's beyond my understanding! The fact that He has chosen our family to proclaim His Word fills me simultaneously with awe and a sense of responsibility. Then, taking inventory of our combined abilities, I am humbled and cannot help but acknowledge

God, because *He* will have to accomplish it. Still, my faith, which is no bigger than a mustard seed, is strengthened by 2 Tim. 3:16, 17 where God promises that His Word will equip everyone who has to accomplish his God-given task.

1 Cor. 3:6, 7 clarifies this partnership between God and His children: *"I planted the seed, Apollos watered it, but God made it grow. So neither he who plants, nor he who waters is anything, but only God who makes things grow."*

The verse at the beginning of this section talks about being chosen to do something specific. What is your calling? Wait on God to reveal it to you and don't try to figure it out yourself.

> Live like children of the living God. Show the world His might. His love is great. He is our God and our Father. I love you, my Lord Jesus and God our Father. Mommy, you have been chosen to prepare the bride. Do you know that Jesus will equip you to manifest His anointing? God will let it happen. He will send you all over the world.

Jesus se ek moet sy woord verkondig en ek sal bly lewe spreek. God wil my gesond maak en ek sal Hom glo weet goos ek gesond word sal ek weer jou bystaan. Sal jy glo dat ek 100% sal weer reg wees. Mamma

God jou leer en leer aan ander mense God sal jou oprig om mense se siele red vir die koningkryk gaan maak self die groot deur oop wat na jou gees gaan.

FRIDAY, FEBRUARY 2, 2007

JESUS SAYS I WILL DECLARE HIS WORD. I HAVE TO KEEP SPEAKING LIFE. GOD WILL HEAL ME AND I BELIEVE HIM. I WILL STAND BY YOU, MOM, LIKE YOU STOOD BY ME, WHEN I'M HEALED. WON'T YOU ALSO BELIEVE THAT I WILL BE 100% HEALED? GOD IS TEACHING YOU, SO THAT YOU CAN TEACH OTHER PEOPLE. GOD IS RAISING YOU UP TO SAVE SOULS OF THE LOST FOR HIS KINGDOM. YOU HAVE TO OPEN THE BIG DOOR TO YOUR SPIRIT.

> PROV. 18:21: THE TONGUE HAS THE POWER OF LIFE AND DEATH, AND THOSE WHO LOVE IT WILL EAT ITS FRUIT.

The importance of the spoken word is illustrated in Ezek. 37. Here God commands the prophet to speak to the dry bones. As he speaks life over the dead bones, they become alive and a mighty army is raised up.

I will never be able to stress this enough. I feel so strongly about it, because I've seen the effects of my words in my own life. When Aldo was in a coma in hospital, I dreamed that his fingers became black and started shriveling. Then Aldo said, "Mommy, speak life over me. Speak life. I was speaking life to his spirit. It doesn't matter if your body is alive after all; if your spirit is dead, you are dead!

There is such power in words. While soft, soothing words bring life, hope and healing, cruel, harsh words reap hopelessness, destruction and death. You only have to listen to what people are saying about each other, to realize the impact their words are having.

What are you saying about your children? If you keep telling them that they are not good enough, pretty enough or clever enough, chances are they'll turn out ugly, stupid and good-for-nothing human beings. As parents you have authority over your children and your words carry even more weight than those of other people. So make sure you pronounce life over them.

Our words have prophetic power. Think also about the things you're saying about your spouse. Husbands, compliment your wives and they will bloom and blossom in front of your very eyes. Wives, praise your husband and you'll always be proud to stand next to him.

My youngest, Josh, already understands the power of words. He often runs up to me saying, "Mommy, they are speaking death!" Even at his young age, he recognizes the negative effects of thoughtless words. But fortunately my children also know the power of positive words. It is the blessing that foils the danger of curses.

Whether you are talking about yourself or voicing an opinion about someone else, your words will have an impact. Perhaps you're eating the sour fruits of your tongue at the moment. Then start speaking life and you'll soon see your situation change.

Let your words work for you instead of against you. The first step is to start listening to yourself. Be aware of what you're saying and you'll be surprised at the ease with which you confess negative thoughts. This is often a sign that you are still in control of your life. I know that whatever I say will stay. Words that roll so easily off your lips, will ultimately determine the quality of your life.

Here are a few biblical examples of how our confessions determine our lives:

❖ Rom. 10:9, 10: "If you confess with your mouth, 'Jesus is Lord,' and believe in your heart that God raised him from the dead, you will be saved. For it is with your heart that you believe and are justified and it is with your mouth that you confess and are saved." – I am saved.

❖ Is. 53:5: "But he was pierced for our transgressions, he was crushed for our iniquities; .... And by his wounds we are healed." – I am healed.

❖ Jn. 8:36: "So if the Son sets you free, you will be free indeed." – I am free.

❖ Rom. 5:5: "...because God has poured out his love into our hearts by the Holy Spirit, whom he has given us." – I can love unconditionally and will never be alone.

❖ Heb. 13:5: "...because God has said, never will I leave you; never will I forsake you." – I can count on God and on His help in my life.

Don't allow the dark shadows of doubt and fear to progress to your tongue. Check your words and speak life!

> Peace for everyone who, like me, is searching for God's presence. May we always be aware of His love and guidance. We'll all be with Him one day.

Lief vir mamma. Ek sien God
op Sy troon en Hy sê Sy Seun
het Sy lewe gegee vir my genesing
Sodoso ek sal gehoorsaam wees
aan God. Sal saam met jou
~~waar~~ bedien ek sal wil sê
Wees weer so lief vir my
soos voor die ongeluk. Sal ons
ons self offer aan God
Gaan en seen God soos ons
Saamin gaan Sy God ontmoet.
Wys my waar gaan ek staan
weet mamma God is saam
se Leermeester. Gaan en
evalueer jou hart of jy Sy
bruid is. God sal jou optel
en self leer soos u

ek kan nie kwaad vir jou word nie!

WEDNESDAY, FEBRUARY 20, 2007

I LOVE YOU, MOMMY. I SEE GOD SITTING ON HIS THRONE. HE SAYS THAT HIS SON GAVE HIS LIFE SO THAT I MIGHT BE HEALED. I WILL OBEY GOD. I WILL SERVE GOD WITH YOU. MOMMY, PLEASE LOVE ME THE WAY YOU DID BEFORE THE ACCIDENT. WON'T WE SACRIFICE OURSELVES TO GOD? WE WILL SEE GOD LIKE SAMUEL SAW GOD. YOU SHOW ME WHERE TO GO. MOMMY, DID YOU KNOW THAT GOD WAS SAMUEL'S TEACHER? TEST YOU HEART AND SEE IF YOU ARE PART OF THE BRIDE. GOD WILL PICK YOU UP AND TEACH YOU HIMSELF.

> 1 JN. 4:8 WHOEVER DOES NOT LOVE, DOES NOT KNOW GOD, BECAUSE GOD IS LOVE.

As Aldo's mother I'm already praying for whoever will be his wife one day. I pray that she will love my son, who is imperfect in the world's eyes, unconditionally. Love, by its very essence, means to accept what is imperfect. The Holy Spirit confirmed this to my heart, but asked, "Retha, I will give her to Aldo, but what about you? Do you love your husband unconditionally?"

Yes, it's so easy to preach to others about how

they should live their lives, but doing it yourself is something else completely.

I started looking at Tinus with new eyes. When I realised that God loved him unconditionally, I wondered why I would ever want to change him.

"If only my husband would change," many women say, "I would love him." Or, "If my husband were more like me, our marriage would be so much better." As if you're so perfect? Perhaps it's because you are still ruling your own life, your relationships and marriage. It was only after I had accepted my partner as the unique creation of God, made by God for His enjoyment, that I could see Tinus through God's eyes. Then I was the one who changed within the trilogy of God, Tinus and I, not my husband.

When God picked me up on that highway after the accident, He accepted me – flaws and pride and all. He didn't demand that I first become perfect or without sin before He would allow me into His presence. Instead He opened His arms and said, "Retha! I have waited so long for you."

The love I have for others impacts directly on my relationship with God. In 1 Jn. 4:16 this is made clear: *"… God is love. Whoever lives in love lives in God, and God in him."*

We all want to be loved unconditionally. We desperately want to be accepted for who we are. Be still then and know that God loves you. He accepts you. He is your protection. Losing your awareness of God's presence in your life is the worst thing that can happen to you.

In order for us to give ourselves to God, we have to protect our hearts more than anything else. That's why we should cultivate the habit of continual prayer. When you're surrounded by His loving presence, you'll never feel alone. After a while, you'll be so tuned in to

Him that you'll feel His presence 24-hours a day. His love will engulf you like a mighty wave and you'll need nothing more.

Don't allow pride to inhibit your relationship with God. Give yourself completely to Him and live in His precious presence.

> Live like children of the living God. Show the world His might. His love is great. He is our God and our Father. I love you, my Lord Jesus and God our Father. Mommy, you have been chosen to prepare the bride. Do you know that Jesus will equip you to manifest His anointing? God will let it happen. He will send you all over the world.

My kop voel lekker
Ek sal gesond word
en nie meer moeilik wees nie
God se ek sal weer reg
praat en dan sal ek
ook sy woord verkondig.
Ek is baie gelukkig
want Julle is so goed
vir my en lief vir my.
Sal jy my asb altyd
so liefhe God gaan
ons saam gebruik om
sy woord te verkondig
Ons is die gelukkigste
gesin. Sal jy asb
ook met my
opnames help
wat ek gaan maak oor Jesus
ek gaan ook CD maak en
vertel dat ek in die hemel was

FRIDAY, NOVEMBER 11, 2005

MY HEAD FEELS GOOD. I WILL BE HEALED AND WON'T BE MOODY ANYMORE. GOD SAYS I WILL REGAIN MY SPEECH COMPLETELY AND I WILL PROCLAIM HIS WORD. I'M VERY HAPPY, BECAUSE YOU TAKE GOOD CARE OF ME AND LOVE ME. WILL YOU ALWAYS LOVE ME LIKE THIS? GOD WILL USE US TOGETHER TO SPREAD THE GOOD NEWS. WE ARE A BLESSED FAMILY. PLEASE MOMMY, WILL YOU HELP ME WITH THE RECORDINGS I'M GOING TO MAKE FOR JESUS? I'M ALSO GOING TO RECORD A CD TO TELL PEOPLE THAT I WENT TO HEAVEN.

REV. 19:12: HIS EYES ARE LIKE BLAZING FIRE, AND ON HIS HEAD ARE MANY CROWNS. HE HAS A NAME WRITTEN ON HIM THAT NO ONE KNOWS BUT HE HIMSELF. HE IS DRESSED IN A ROBE DIPPED IN BLOOD AND HIS NAME IS THE WORD OF GOD.

In our everyday existence, God's Word is the lamp unto our feet and the light on our way. Jesus is the Word of God. Although there's certainly nothing wrong with reading Christian literature, the Bible is certainly the most important book of all, and that's why we should spend more time reading it than we do anything else.

The Truth in the Word of God sets me free! My self image is often based on my emotions and they are flawed and false, but when I read the Bible I see myself through God's eyes and I can use it to set the course for my life. For me it basically came down to who and what I wanted to believe: God or my emotions.

Keeping a vigil at Aldo's bedside while he was in a coma, I found it very difficult to remain positive and to speak life (whether out loud or in quiet prayer) while everyone was making negative pronouncements about his condition and prognosis. One day I just couldn't take it anymore. I fell on my face before God and told Him that I am taking Him at His Word. I started speaking the Word, actual Scripture verses, instead of my thoughts and feelings, and things started changing. When you speak the Word of God in faith, your circumstances *will* change, as it changed for the Nigerian pastor who was dead for four days. His wife stood firm on the Word of God and the Truth resurrected him to life.

Although I still heard many negative pronouncements about Aldo, I knew that God's Word was the Truth and the Truth has dominion over medical facts and results. God spoke to me about Aldo, and I believe Him wholeheartedly.

The more time I spent in the Word, the more answers I got. God was speaking to me. He still speaks to us through nature, people, dreams, and visions and through His Spirit. God didn't fall silent after biblical times. Stay in and study the Scriptures. Ask the Holy Spirit of Truth to reveal and explain the Word of God and He will speak to you too. The Bible is our source of strength.

You can trust the Word of God. If He said it, it will be done. God promises in Is. 55:11: *"So the word that goes out from my mouth; it will not return to me empty, but will accomplish what I desire and achieve the purpose for which I sent it."*

When God speaks to us through His Word (and if we accept it in faith!) things will change. I chose to believe His Word over the medical opinions and to look at the cross instead of my circumstances.

What you sow, you will reap. Life is like an echo. Whatever you scream into the chasm of life, will come back to you. In other words, what you put in, you will get out too. If you spend a lot of time with your family, you will have a strong relationship with every member and you'll receive that as a reward on the time you invested with them. Similarly the state of your marriage reflects the time you spend with your spouse. I guess the real question is how much time you are spending in the Word of God, because *that* determines what your relationship with Him is like. Perhaps you are currently reaping a harvest that you wished you'd never sowed. It's not too late to change.

Your ignorance of the Word can cause you to miss out on the fullness of God. You only have one life to live. Live it in the Word.

Jesus sal ons pappa seen en ons
sal kom [illegible] want ons sal wees
soos n boum wat geplant is by waterstrome.
Jesus se Ek gaan en sy woord verkondig
oor die wereld.
Sal jy saam gaan na waar ek
gestuur gaan word
Jesus sey my self en stuur
wees voorbereid
Jesus se gaan en werk vir
my ek sal vir jou sorg.
Word die Rekha wat Ek beplan
het vir jou jy gaan groot bediening he
oor die wereld.

TUESDAY, JUNE 21, 2005

JESUS WILL BLESS MY DADDY AND WE WILL LOVE HIM, BECAUSE HE IS LIKE A TREE THAT IS PLANTED BY A STREAM. JESUS SAYS I WILL PROCLAIM HIS WORD ALL OVER THE WORLD. WILL YOU GO WITH ME WHEREVER HE SENDS ME? JESUS WILL ANOINT ME AND SEND ME. PREPARE FOR IT. JESUS HAS A MESSAGE FOR YOU, MOMMY. HE SAYS, "GO AND WORK FOR ME AND I WILL TAKE CARE OF YOU. BE THE RETHA THAT I CREATED YOU TO BE, BECAUSE I DESTINED YOU TO HAVE A LARGE MINISTRY ACROSS THE WORLD.

EPH. 6:13: THEREFORE PUT ON THE FULL ARMOR OF GOD, SO THAT WHEN THE DAY OF EVIL COMES, YOU MAY BE ABLE TO STAND YOUR GROUND.

There is a reason why God gave us His armour: we have to use it when we battle against evil. Without the protection of the armour of God, we are naked and defenceless in the spiritual realm; sitting ducks for the enemy. God protects us from danger, helps us in a crisis and confirms our divine calling. Let's take a closer look at God's dress code:

❖ The belt of truth around our waist is vital. It protects us against the lies and falsehood that the devil uses to destroy our faith in God and His promises. Your belt keeps your pants up. Without the belt of truth, you might get caught with your spiritual pants around your ankles. Buckle up and be prepared.

❖ The breastplate of righteousness refers to the fact that we were put in rightstanding with God through the blood of Jesus. He vindicated us morally and restored us in God's eyes. The breastplate thus is our righteousness through Jesus Christ and that's why it protects our most vulnerable part: our hearts that was made innocent of sin and holy through the cross.

❖ Our shoes are eager and ready to go wherever He sends us to spread the Good News in peace. This refers to our willingness to evangelize the world. Are you willing to go to China, Russia or some other African country to spread the Word of God over the globe? Will you give up your comfortable life and everyone you hold dear to go to a strange country, where there might not be freedom of religion, to live and work among people who might betray you to the prosecuting authority at any time? Are you at least willing to pray for and contribute money towards those who will answer this most important call?

Even if God doesn't ask you to go to Korea or the Middle East, are you willing to testify about God's goodness in your life at your workplace, in your circle of friends or at your children's school? When you put your shoes on tomorrow, think about all the places they will take you and the opportunities you'll have to tell people that Jesus is alive!

❖ The shield of faith deflects the burning arrows of the enemy. As gold is purified and tested in fire, so too is our faith in God. Just because you believe in

God's Word, and His promises, it doesn't mean that you won't experience doubt. This is the time to lift up your shield of faith to withstand the enemy. A practical way to do this is to phone someone who also walks in faith and ask them to pray for you.

When the enemy attacks you, go to your Bible. Reread the promises and Scriptures that the Holy Spirit has shared with you over the years. Read it out loud. Hearing the powerful Word of God will give you faith and you'll withstand the enemy.

❖ The helmet of salvation protects our heads and with it our minds. We put it on when we acknowledge our sin and it is secured when we accept Jesus' atonement as the free gift of grace.

Beheading someone is a sure way of killing him and that's why salvation is likened to a helmet: It protects the most crucial part of your body from the enemy. You might still survive an injury to your leg or arm, but if you lose your head, you're done for. So secure that helmet. Confess with your mouth that you are saved through grace and the enemy's attack will be foiled.

❖ The sword of the Spirit is used to withstand and slay the enemy. The Word of God is a powerful and mighty weapon that is sharper than any sword and can test the thoughts and depths of the heart. To the Christian, it is jewel and the distinctive of mark God.

Whether you are doing grief counselling or giving advice on how to handle rebellious teenagers, rely on God's Word. No clever quote or 5-point action plan can defeat the enemy of grief or rebellion (or any other enemy) like the Word of God. Try to commit at least a few key Scriptures to memory, so that you can quote it when necessary. But don't worry if you can't remember the exact words: The Holy Spirit will give you the right words to say.

❖ Continual prayer in the Spirit makes us vigilant. It is our direct communications line with God and is strengthened by thanksgiving and praise.

We have to put on these special pieces of spiritual clothing, not only that we can stand our ground during the fight, but that we might also have the victory in Christ Jesus.

> Now today, I'll be what Jesus wants me to be. I have to be a prophet who warns people that Jesus is coming back for us. We will experience the power of the God we serve through floods and earthquakes. Mom, will you warn everyone that the floods are coming?

God will help me not to hurt you again, Mommy. I don't want to hurt you. Please forgive me.

God wants me to preach His word, like you do, Mommy. I will go with you to your next appearance. You have to go to church from now on to see how you should act. God and some of the angels will be there. Raphael will also be there. Please take me with you when you go there. I see Raphael at night when he comes to speak to me. It's his job to heal us. He helped me to regain my sight. He will also heal me from my other injuries.

Laat ons soos Jesus gaan
en die woord verkondig
Ek weet ek gaan gou gesond
wees om sy woord te verkondig
Sal jou gees oop gemaak
wees vir God se gees
om in te kom. Hy wil
jou gebruik om mense
te vertel van die HG
en hoe om Hom aan te
neem. Soos Sameul sal ek
ook terug gaan na
die tempel. God sal my
self leer deur die HG
wat by my is elke
oomblik. Leef
soos God wil he herlig
ek weet ek gaan 100% gesond
wees - wees geduldig mamma
wees geduldig. Lief jou
en pappa.

Engel
Raphaél

TUESDAY, OCTOBER 25, 2005

LET US GO OUT LIKE JESUS DID, AND PROCLAIM THE WORD. I JUST KNOW I'M GOING TO BE HEALED SOON SO THAT I CAN START PROCLAIMING THE WORD. WILL YOUR SPIRIT BE OPEN SO THAT GOD'S SPIRIT CAN COME IN? GOD SAYS, "I WANT TO USE YOU TO TELL PEOPLE ABOUT THE HOLY SPIRIT AND HOW TO ACCEPT HIM." LIKE SAMUEL, I TOO WILL RETURN TO THE TEMPLE. GOD WILL TEACH ME ALL I NEED TO KNOW THROUGH THE HOLY SPIRIT WHO IS WITH ME CONSTANTLY. LIVE THE WAY GOD WANTS YOU TO: HOLY. I KNOW I WILL BE 100% HEALED. BE PATIENT, MOMMY! I LOVE, MOMMY AND DADDY.

BEAR FRUIT

MT. 7: 20: THUS BY THEIR FRUIT, YOU WILL RECOGNISE THEM.

God spoke to me and said, "Retha, you are like the fig tree. It's beautiful and big with a sturdy stem and huge leaves, but there is no fruit. You've even put up signs all around the tree; 'I'm a Christian!' 'Look at me, the Christian.' You're in church every Sunday, but where is your fruit? Instead of bearing fruit, you're always criticizing and judging others, tearing them down.

"Resist the temptation of judging others at all costs, because I will use the same measure you're using for them, to judge you. By judging others, you force Me to judge you and in this way you've opened the door for Satan to pollute your spirit. Instead of judging others, I want you to bless them. Bless them continuously.

"Allow the Holy Spirit to prune your life and root out this critical spirit. Don't get on your high horse when you're being pruned. Be still and know that I am God and I am in control of the pruning process too. This is how an adult child of Mine reacts to pruning."

It was a tough word for me, but I had to allow Him to cut away whatever was not of Him. Do you also sometimes rebel when the Gardener approaches with the pruning scissors? God wants us to bear fruit so that he may feed the world with us. Pruning makes the tree bear more fruit and thus we too have to be pruned so that the fruits of the spirit will become evident in our lives.

Gal. 5:22 and 23 tell us exactly which spiritual fruits God expects His children to bear: *"....love, joy, peace, patience, kindness, goodness, faithfulness, gentleness and self-control..."*

When the Holy Spirit lives in us, we will reveal His character through these fruits.

Jesus says we will proclaim His Word along with other families. We will see God. Go and tell the truth that Jesus lives! Become what God wants you to be: holy and obedient to Him. Will you always work for Him, Mommy? We know that He lives, because we were with Jesus in the throne room. He will heal me. He will make me over, as if from clay, He will make me – a new creation by His hand and to His honor.

Jy moet soos waarsku so gaan
Lewens verander waarom God
wil hê dat jy mense moet
waarsku dat Hy oppad is
wees gereed as Hy ons
kom haal. Daar is 'n
Bruilofsfees wat wag vir almal
wat gereed is. Lees Math. 25

Lief vir u Jesus en dankie
dat u vir my gesterf het!!
Lief vir u Gees van God
gooi alles in jou huis uit
wat nie van God is nie.
Weet mamma dat jy geroep
is vir God self en dat
jy net vir Hom moet leef
Wie sal gaan en sy woord
verkondig God sal my
gesond maak en ek sal Hom
dien solank ek leef.

MONDAY, FEBRUARY 26, 2007

YOU HAVE TO WARN PEOPLE, MOMMY. THAT'S HOW LIVES WILL CHANGE. GOD WANTS YOU TO WARN PEOPLE THAT HE IS ON HIS WAY BACK. BE READY. HE IS COMING BACK FOR US. THE WEDDING FEAST IS PREPARED AND WAITING FOR THOSE WHO ARE READY. READ MATTHEW 25. I LOVE YOU, LORD JESUS. THANK YOU FOR DYING FOR ME. I LOVE YOU SPIRIT OF THE LORD. GET RID OF EVERYTHING IN YOUR HOUSE THAT IS NOT OF THE LORD. MOMMY, DO YOU KNOW THAT YOU ARE CALLED OF GOD AND YOU HAVE TO LIVE YOUR LIFE SOLELY FOR HIM. WHO WILL GO AND PREACH HIS WORD? GOD WILL HEAL ME AND I WILL SERVE HIM AS LONG AS I LIVE.

> ACTS 1:8: BUT YOU WILL RECEIVE POWER WHEN THE HOLY SPIRIT COMES ON YOU; AND YOU WILL BE MY WITNESSES IN JERUSALEM, AND IN SAMARIA, AND TO THE ENDS OF THE EARTH.

I'm viewed as an expert in the fields of image and appearance. I know all the secrets to unlocking physical beauty and presenting a spotless outward appearance. However, as my relationship with God intensified, I became aware of the weaknesses in my spiritual attire. Although God has given me the courage of a lion, and has convinced me that Aldo and I will be able to fulfil His task, I still felt like I needed more skills:

"Lord, I'll need a lot of guidance. Please help me!"

God's answer to this was simple: "I want you to walk in the way of righteousness. You have My Spirit in you and the Spirit will equip you with all you need to know."

Then God gave me two pieces of Scripture that confirms this. The first is in Rom. 8: 9-10: *"You are controlled ....by the Spirit, if the Spirit of God lives in you. And if anyone does not have the Spirit of Christ, he does not belong to Christ."* Secondly, Jn. 14:26: *"But the Counsellor, the Holy Spirit, whom the Father will send in my name, will teach you all things and will remind you of everything I have said to you".*

If you want to be filled with the Holy Spirit you have to empty out your heart; throw out all your agendas, your dreams, needs and plans. Get rid of your own stubborn will. Once you've emptied yourself of yourself in this way, God's Spirit will fill you completely and equip you for whatever He wants to accomplish through you.

It is easy to recognize someone who lives in the Spirit. He is God-centered instead of self-centered. A spirit-filled person has died unto himself and has accepted the mercy of a new life in Christ. Every aspect of his life is guided by the Spirit, who enables him to fulfill the specific plan that God has with his life.

God revealed to me just how vital it is to be filled with the Holy Spirit when I went jogging around the boat club at Hartebeespoortdam one evening. I stopped to catch my breath at the marina and saw the boats anchored to the shore. They were making a click-click sound as they bobbed calmly on the surface.

"It's lovely, isn't it?"

"Yes Lord. The clinking sound is soothing too."

"These boats are like My church. Sunday after

Sunday they stand in churches clicking together. Some click more loudly than others, but click, they click! What, do you think, do these boats need to achieve their full potential?" He asked.

"These are sail boats and they need wind."

"My wind must blow through My church if they are going to be all I created them to be. They have to be filled with My Spirit."

After the ascension, the disciples waited and prayed for 10 days before they were filled with the Holy Spirit and only *after* they were filled with the Spirit did they start teaching and testifying as Jesus said that they would. Without the Holy Spirit, we are lost. Each person who wants to live for God and do His bidding has to be filled with the Spirit to be used by Him.

None of us are holy. Unconfessed sins, bad habits, and an unforgiving heart hinder the work of the Spirit in our lives. That's why the spirit-filled person listens to the Spirit and uproots these intruders so that God can finish the work He has started through us.

When the Holy Spirit dwells in us, He will work in us so that we will come to resemble Jesus more and more. Although there are many character traits that the Spirit cultivates in us, He has taught me seven of these. They are...

* THE SPIRIT OF PRAYER
* THE SPIRIT OF SONSHIP
* THE SPIRIT OF OBEDIENCE
* THE SPIRIT OF FAITH
* THE SPIRIT OF WORSHIP
* THE SPIRIT OF TRUTH
* THE SPIRIT OF COVENANT

Aan al my maats

Jesus het my lewe gered.
Jesus wil ons lewe gebruik tot
Sy eer. Ons moet Hom net eer.
Dankie dat julle vir my gebid
het. Jesus het vir my gese julle
bid vir my. Hy was trots op julle omdat
julle op Hom vertrou het.

MONDAY, MARCH 6, 2006

TO ALL MY FRIENDS,
JESUS SAVED MY LIFE! JESUS WANTS TO USE OUR LIVES TO HIS HONOUR. WE HAVE TO HONOR HIM. THANK YOU ALL FOR PRAYING FOR ME. JESUS TOLD ME YOU PRAYED FOR ME. HE WAS PROUD OF YOU FOR TRUSTING IN HIM.

ROM. 8:26-27: ... THE SPIRIT HELPS US IN OUR WEAKNESS. WE DO NOT KNOW WHAT WE OUGHT TO PRAY FOR, BUT THE SPIRIT HIMSELF INTERCEDES FOR US WITH GROANS THAT WORDS CANNOT EXPRESS.

I've already indicated the many different ways in which God speaks to us. But we can only speak to God in one way and that is through prayer. All the great men and women from the Bible, the prophets and disciples all "prayed continually" (1 Thes. 5:17). Note in the gospels how Jesus always goes off to pray before we see Him work a miracle. We cannot doubt that prayer is of paramount importance in our relationship with God.

Most people feel they don't know how to pray, but if we remain in the Spirit, He will teach us *how* to pray and even *who* to pray for, because the Holy Spirit is the Spirit of supplication. We just have to be sensitive to Him. How often had you thought of someone all day and in your spirit you knew you should pray for him, but you just didn't? Only to find out later that he really needed prayer at that time in his life.

Tinus and the kids picked me up after a speaking engagement in Secunda (Mpumalanga) one day. Aldo, who couldn't speak at that time, wrote that we had to pray for a family friend. Because Aldo insisted, we stopped and prayed for him. Aldo sat with his eyes closed all the way home and I could see that he was praying in his spirit. Later he took my cellphone and indicated that I should phone our friend, but I didn't, thinking that Aldo was just being head-strong. Days later, when I finally called, I was shocked to hear that our friend had truly needed our prayers that day because he had been in a motor car accident. Although he wasn't hurt, other people died on the scene. Surely the Spirit of supplication was working through Aldo when he asked us to pray for our friend that day.

In Mt. 7:7 God promises, *"Ask and it will be given to you; seek and you will find; knock and the door will be opened to you,"* and in Mt. 21:22 He reiterates, *"If you believe, you will receive whatever you ask for in prayer".* Two fantastic promises, each revealing the importance of prayer. The problem is that most of us think that to "ask", "seek" and "pray" is a five minute deal. You won't receive anything if you only spend the last five minutes of your day, with God in prayer just before you fall asleep, utterly exhausted. Prayer that moves mountains, brings healing and spiritual maturity demands commitment, and time to wait on God. You have to seek God like Jacob did: holding on to Him until He blesses you. In our fast-paced world we just don't have the time to wait on God and this is where the enemy steals from us. When we pray, we just rattle off a list of our needs and wants and then we get up and leave His presence without having received His peace or joy.

Instead God wants to build an intimate and loving relationship with you through prayer. It is your direct communications channel to God and you can access

Him anywhere any time. One night I worked late in my office and on my way to bed around one a.m., I checked on Aldo. I found him on his knees.

"Aldo, you have to go to sleep now. You have school in the morning," I said rather sternly.

"I'm waiting on God, Mommy," he replied.

I left his room with tears in my eyes. I realized then that the way I taught him to pray, when he was younger, was so wrong: It was something along the lines of, "Tell God what you need, say 'Amen' and jump into bed." Surely this cannot please God.

God wants us to live in a continuous state of prayer. If you persist in prayer, He will reveal Himself to you. Jer. 33:3 says, *"Call to me and I will answer you and tell you great and unsearchable things you do not know".* This taught me that prayer isn't a one-way street. Now, when I'm finished praying, I wait on God to hear His voice.

"Mommy, do you still pray for me?" asked Aldo before school one day.

"Of course I do," I answered. "And I won't stop praying for you. Why would you even ask me this?"

"When I was in heaven I saw that God would send an angel to help the people whenever someone prayed. So please don't stop praying for me."

Moments like these make me humble, but I take heart knowing what is written in 1 Pet. 5:5-6: *"... clothe yourselves with humility ... because God opposes the proud, but gives grace to the humble. Humble yourselves, therefore under God's mighty hand, that he may lift you up in due time."* And so I bend my stiff knees and bow my proud back, knowing just how dependent I am on Him.

"Remember Retha, the moment you leave my presence, you will be walking in your own self-sufficiency and pride again," God said. "There is humility in my presence."

"Yes Lord, and peace and joy and love," I added.

as julle my nie geoffer
het nie was ek dood.

Weet jy dat ek was
die heeltyd by Jesus
waar Hy my heeltyd sy
woord geleer het. God het
weer my lewend gemaak
en sy gees in my geblaas holy breat

SATURDAY, OCTOBER 15, 2005

IF YOU HADN'T SACRIFICED ME, I'D BE DEAD. MOMMY, DID YOU KNOW THAT I WAS WITH GOD ALL THE TIME? HE TAUGHT ME HIS WORD WHEN I WAS IN HEAVEN. GOD BROUGHT ME BACK TO LIFE BY BLOWING HIS SPIRIT INTO ME. IT WAS A HOLY BREAK.

> ROM. 8:15: FOR YOU DID NOT RECEIVE A SPIRIT THAT MAKES YOU A SLAVE AGAIN TO FEAR, BUT YOU RECEIVED THE SPIRIT OF SONSHIP. AND BY HIM WE CRY, 'ABBA, FATHER'.

We've all felt rejected at some point in our lives. You may have felt as if you didn't belong anywhere; as if you were completely alone in this world with no one to care for you. You just feel empty inside. So you try to fill this emptiness with all sorts of things like new shiny cars, luxurious houses, designer clothes and expensive holidays, hoping that you'll be accepted because of these achievements. But still, the void remains.

I was like that too, always searching for something to make me feel whole. Now I know that only God's love and acceptance can truly fill that emptiness inside.

Now that I've given my life to Him, I can truly say that I *belong* to Him. God has accepted me. He chose me even though I was proud and full of myself. He called me out of darkness and into His marvelous light. I became His through the Spirit who makes us sons and daughters of the Most High. And I know He will never reject me, even if I sometimes still fail Him. I fit in with Him and with His people. The Bible tells me that He wrote my name in the book of life and on the palm of His hand.

In the mornings before Josh leaves for school, I often draw a heart with a smiley face in the palm of his five-year-old little hand and then do the same in my hand. "Whenever you look at it, you will know how much I love you and that I'm thinking of you all day long," I would say.

While it is terrific to know that we belong to God, it requires something on our part too. We have to live a Holy life. Eph. 1:4, 5 explains this in no uncertain terms: *"For he chose us in him before the creation of the world to be holy and blameless in his sight. In love he predestined us to be adopted as his sons through Jesus Christ, in accordance with his pleasure and will."* Again it is clear that we are saved through grace and became His children through the work of Jesus Christ on the cross, but it demands of us to be "holy and blameless" at the same time.

The fact is that you cannot say that you belong to God, if you're still in control of you own life! You have to give up your life as a living sacrifice to Him. In Mt. 16:24, 25 Jesus says, *"...if anyone would come after me, he must deny himself and take up his cross and follow me. For whoever wants to save his life will lose it, but whoever loses his life for me, will find it"*. We have to give up everything that we hold dear in this world. That is the prerequisite to becoming His heir. I had to sacrifice my son, as well as all my Christian doctrine and ways of serving God. As long as you think that you can provide for yourself, you will never receive the full blessing of Pentecost. You have to lay down your emotions, your thoughts, your heart and most of all your own will. Only then will God fill you with His Spirit, and can you live in the Spirit. It is a radical and life-changing choice, and although it is not easy, the reward for this sacrifice is eternal life.

After the accident, I have come to realize that nothing in my life is *too* precious to sacrifice to God. It has taught me that God sometimes uses the crisis in our lives to get us to the point where we are willing to lay down our lives. Only when we are this 'sold out' to Him, can we be His hands and feet to the world. God trusts me with His work, because He doesn't rely on my strengths and abilities, but on the indestructible seed of faith that was implanted in me through the Holy Spirit when I was reborn in Christ.

God shows us every day how much He loves and accepts us.

We've started a new tradition in our house whereby we take turns at the dinner table to tell how each of us experienced God's love that day. Since we've started doing this, we look for evidence of His love everywhere. Nowadays our food is cold before we are through testifying about His goodness.

When you remain in the Spirit, you cannot focus on your own problems. Instead you're focused on His love and acceptance.

Jesus sgaan ons gebruik om sy woord te verkondig.
Saam sal ons sy glory beleef.
Jy moet gaan en die mense vertel you dat Jesus lewe.
Wil jy God se glory beleef
IMPORTANT
Wees soos wat Jesus jou wil hê heilig net vir Hom.
Wees gehoorsaam aan sy stem. God sal jou wys wat om te sê op die kamp.

TUESDAY, JANUARY 23, 2007

JESUS WILL USE US TO PROCLAIM HIS WORD. TOGETHER WE WILL SEE HIS GLORY. MOM, YOU HAVE TO TELL EVERYONE THAT JESUS IS ALIVE! DO YOU WANT TO SEE GOD'S GLORY? THEN BE HOLY UNTO HIM. OBEY HIS VOICE AND HE WILL GIVE YOU THE RIGHT WORDS TO SPEAK.

> 1 PET. 1:2: WHO HAVE BEEN CHOSEN ACCORDING TO THE FOREKNOWLEDGE OF GOD THE FATHER, THROUGH THE SANCTIFYING WORK OF THE SPIRIT, FOR OBEDIENCE TO JESUS CHRIST...

When you enthrone God and hand over control of your life to Him, it is a sincere surrender, not an emotional or impulsive decision that can be easily reversed. One of the implications of this decision is that you *want* to obey God. And that is what He expects from us too. He wants you to obey Him in all and everything. You cannot choose to obey Him in one aspect of your life, while you do whatever you please in another. It's all or nothing with God. There are no grey areas.

In 1 Sam. 15:22 we see just how strongly God feels about obedience: "Does the Lord delight in burnt offerings and sacrifices as much as in obeying the voice of the Lord? To obey is better than sacrifice, and to heed is better than the fat of rams."

I've had to learn this lesson the hard way. Although I served God, I wasn't sold out to Him and it took this tragedy for me to surrender my life. I first had to hold my child's broken body in my arms, and later learn to live with his crippled walk before I stopped trying to do His will in my own strength. Once you know how much you really need God; how desperately dependent you are on Him, it becomes easy to obey Him.

My whole life I've tried to obey God, because I was afraid of Him. I was afraid that if I made a mistake, He would punish me and that's why I tried to do the right thing, not because I *wanted* to obey Him. Only now do I realize that to obey Him is to love Him. Jesus says in Jn. 14:21, *"Whoever has my commands and obeys them, he is the one who loves me. He who loves me will be loved by my Father, and I too will love him and show myself to him".* Many precious children of God feel that their relationship with Him has stagnated. I want to challenge you to obey God more and more and He will reveal Himself to you in new ways.

Perhaps you look at me and say, "She doesn't have a choice. She has to cling to God and obey Him. She's just trying to make the best of a really bad situation." But this is not so. I've discovered that happiness (or unhappiness) has little to do with circumstances. It is about knowing, obeying and loving God.

The Bible teaches us that we are joint heirs with the Son of God. Thus He cannot but expect the same degree of obedience from us as He did from Jesus. In Phil. 2:8 we see Jesus as the obedient servant of God: *"And being found in appearance as a man, he humbled himself and became obedient to death – even death on a cross!"*

Word Heilig soos God wil he
jy moet wees. soos God lewe
so sal jy sy krag sien ook
en jou lewe sal sy krag manifesteer

Be holy, since God expects you to be holy. If you live a holy life you will see and manifest His power.

Be prepared for Jesus' return. I will obey God like Samson did. What will we say when we are standing before the throne in heaven one day? I long to go back to heaven.

God sal jou uit jou omstandighede uithaal. God het jou so lief en jy moet net jou lewe aan Hom offer. God het jou so lief daarom het Hy Sy Seun gestuur vir jou. God sal jou omstandigheid verander, glo net in God, maak jou lewe oop aan God. Hy sal ons die weg wys wat ons moet wandel. Word wat God van jou vra, 'n mens wat gesterf het in jouself. Glo in God en onthou...

Jesus leef, ek het Hom gesien in die hemel. Leef vir Hom.

Liefde Aldo

24 Julie 2006

Monday, July 24, 2006

God will save you from your circumstances. God loves you very much. All you have to do in return is to give Him your life. God loves you so much, that He sent His Son for you. God will change your circumstances. You just have to have faith in Him. Open up your life to God. He will show us the way. Become what God wants you to be: someone who has died unto himself. Believe in God and remember: Jesus is alive! I saw Him in heaven. Live for Him.

> 2 Cor. 4:13: It is written: I believed; therefore I have spoken. With that same spirit of faith we also believe and therefore speak.

One of the best days of my life was the day Aldo told us how God had restored him to life. "I was dead, but then God blew His Spirit into me and the next moment I was alive." I often think about this when I contemplate those who breathe in and out, but who are spiritually dead.

The moment you are reborn, God blows the Spirit of faith into your nose, just like He blew physical life into the body of man when He first created Him. It's this Ruah (literally breath of God) that gives life!

Since the accident, I've come to appreciate the power of faith. God promised me that He would heal Aldo and I'm clinging to it, deliberately focusing on His promise and ensuring that my actions don't contradict it. The enemy, who knows how dangerous we can be if we're faith-filled, is always trying to focus our minds on the negative aspects of a situation, hoping that we will succumb to fear. This happens to me when people ask me how long I'm going to close my eyes to the reality of Aldo's condition. My answer to this is that I'll believe God is going to heal him until I die. I will keep believing, because I know it's the only thing that will ever please God.

Satan still comes to me with his fear and disbelief, but I've learnt to recognize him now. He usually speaks through people and often it is through people who are close to me. This is when I concentrate on looking with my spirit eyes and recite 2 Cor. 5:7, *"We live by faith, not by sight"*. Just like Abraham, I will hope against hope and I will receive the promise. Faith is about seeing with your heart and believing in things we cannot see with our physical eyes. When I was in the throne room, God asked me how I saw Aldo in my mind's eye. Like every mother, I visualized my son being healthy and happy, playing soccer with his friends. But God had a different vision.

"I will give you more than what you could ever ask or imagine," He said.

If you ask me what *my* definition of faith is, I'll have to say it's the willingness to trust God although you *don't* know the answers. It is to say, "No matter what, Lord, I will trust in You". And it is not easy to make this declaration. One day, out of the blue, Aldo asked, "Mommy, if Jesus were to return today, would He find even one person on Earth who still believes?"

As for me, I look for the smallest improvement in Aldo's condition to strengthen my faith and I praise God for it, because I know every huge work started out small.

> Are we becoming God's bride? Please teach me to wait on God, Mommy. He will heal me in His time.

Hy het gese ek sal oor die wereld gaan
en van Hom vertel.
Jesus is baie lief vir my.
Jesus is ook baie lief vir julle.
Jesus is ook baie lief vir Josh.
baie dankie Jesus
dat jy my lewe gered het.
Jesus prys U naam.
Jesus ons eer U naam.

THURSDAY, 29 DECEMBER, 2005

HE SAID THAT I WOULD TRAVEL THE WORLD AND TELL PEOPLE ABOUT HIM. JESUS LOVES ME VERY MUCH. JESUS ALSO LOVES EVERY ONE OF YOU. JESUS LOVES JOSH. THANK YOU, LORD JESUS, FOR SAVING MY LIFE. PRAISE THE NAME OF JESUS. JESUS, WE HONOR YOUR NAME.

JH. 4:24: GOD IS SPIRIT, AND HIS WORSHIPERS MUST WORSHIP IN SPIRIT AND IN TRUTH.

When the Spirit of God dwells in you, you will have an intense desire to worship Him. Worshipping may be somewhat of an abstract concept, but it comes down to showing a deep respect and love for God. It goes hand in hand with praising, sacrificing and honouring Him. Since these activities are 100% God-centered, you can't truly worship God until you've died to yourself. Then the Holy Spirit will lead you and direct you in your worship.

We need to worship God daily as this is where we find the power we need to stand against the evil forces in the spiritual realm (Eph. 6:12). When we worship God in the Spirit, we are praising Him in a way that we cannot do in the flesh. In 2 Chr. 20 we read about an impending battle between Judah and her enemies. But instead of sharpening their swords, we read about their praise and worship. Time after time the prophet tells them, *"Do not be afraid or discouraged,... for the battle is not yours but God's"* and then we see the people's reaction to this in verses 18,19 and 21: *"... and all the people of Judah and Jerusalem fell down in worship before the Lord, ...stood up and praised the Lord, the God of Israel with a loud voice....to sing to the Lord and to praise him for the splendour of his holiness.... saying: "give thanks to the LORD for his love endures forever.'"*

It's important for us to note here that they are rejoicing, *not* so much in the fact that God delivered them from their enemies, but in *who* He is. They are praising His character, His loving, gracious nature. This is the key to worshipping God. We must worship Him for *who* He is. If we focus on Him, it is possible for us to praise Him even in adverse circumstances, even in times when things are not going so well for us. If you feel overwhelmed by whatever is happening in your life, it's time to worship God for being in control of your out-of-control situation. If you are ill, praise Him for being your Healer. If you are in financial need, praise Him for being your Provider. I don't care how bad things are in your life, you can *always* praise Him for loving you first, for giving His life for you so that you might escape death and have life, for giving you His Holy Spirit to guide you, and for the knowledge that He hasn't given up on you yet!

Praising God for Himself is the heart of worship and it will bring you closer to Him than anything else. When you worship Him in the Spirit, focusing on Him alone, His glory will come upon you like a precious wedding gown. It will envelop you completely and if physical eyes would be able to see it, it would seem like a fire around you. To experience the glory of God like this, is to be desired more than anything else on Earth.

After my quiet time one night, God asked me to bring Him a sacrifice of praise. Instantly tears started rolling down my cheeks as I had to admit that I had never before brought my King a sacrifice of praise. My back had always been too stiff to bow down to Him, and decorum has always prevented me from shouting in celebration of Him! God wants to be adored like this. He says in Lk. 19:40, *"... if they keep quiet, the stones will cry out!"*

I want to encourage you today to take the initiative and cast off all your preconceived ideas about worship. Let's bow down to Him, lift up our hands and shout with the angels, *"Holy, holy, holy, is the Lord God Almighty..."* (Rev. 4:8).

He is worthy of this spirit-filled worship!

Aan almal wat ook Jesus se teenwoordigheid saam met my soek. Wees gereed as Hy ons kom haal. Dit gaan vinniger wees as wat ons dink. Sal jy Hom asb. aanneem want anders sal jy hel toe gaan. Doen dit asb. gou! Jy het nog 'n kans. Jesus het die volmaakte prys betaal vir jou en my. Hy het my alles gewys in die Hemel en ook die hel. Glo my jy wil nie hel toe gaan nie! Sal jy nou Jesus aanneem asb. Jesus het jou so lief, glo my asb. Jy is die rede waarom Hy my terug gestuur het. Ek wou nie terug gekom het nie. Maar Hy wil hê jy moet reg wees.

TUESDAY, 12 SEPTEMBER, 2006

BE PREPARED FOR WHEN HE COMES BACK FOR US. IT WILL HAPPEN SOONER THAN WE THINK. WON'T YOU PLEASE ACCEPT HIM AS YOUR PERSONAL SAVIOUR? IF YOU DON'T, YOU WILL GO TO HELL. PLEASE DO IT SOON WHILE YOU STILL HAVE THE CHANCE TO DO IT. JESUS HAS ALREADY PAID THE COMPLETE PRICE FOR YOU AND ME. HE SHOWED ME EVERYTHING IN HEAVEN AND IN HELL. BELIEVE ME WHEN I SAY, YOU DON'T WANT TO GO TO HELL. PLEASE, WON'T YOU ACCEPT JESUS RIGHT NOW? JESUS LOVES YOU SO MUCH, BELIEVE ME. YOU ARE THE REASON WHY HE SENT ME BACK. I DIDN'T WANT TO COME BACK, BUT HE SENT ME BACK SO THAT YOU CAN BE READY FOR HIS RETURN.

> JN. 15:26: WHEN THE COUNSELLOR COMES.... THE SPIRIT OF TRUTH WHO GOES OUT FROM THE FATHER, HE WILL TESTIFY ABOUT ME.

When we accept Jesus Christ as our personal Savior, God expects us to live a life of truth, because it is one of His defining characteristics. In fact, Jesus declares in Jn. 14:6 that truth is His middle name when He says, *"... 'I am the way and the truth and the life. No one comes to the Father except through me'".*

So if we are to be His children, the truth ought to be evident in everything we do. In direct opposition to God, who is the epitome of truth, the devil is called *" ... a liar and the father of lies"* (Jn. 8:44). Whenever you tell a so-called white lie, or lie by omission, you are aligning yourself with evil.

The Spirit of truth is at work when we counsel others with their problems. We, as human beings, don't have all the answers and we might not know what to say or how to advise someone. This is where the Holy Spirit of truth will give you the right words to say. *"If any of you lacks wisdom, he should ask God who gives generously to all without finding fault, and it will be given to him."* – Jas. 1:5.

The Spirit of truth is of great help when we read the Bible. It is sometimes difficult to understand Scripture, or we may be unclear as to what God wants to reveal to us with a specific piece of Scripture and how it applies to our circumstances. Then it is necessary to pray that God's Spirit of truth will open our minds and give us insight so that we may understand. The Psalmist had the same prayer in Ps. 25:5: *"guide me in your truth and teach me..."* The Bible also states time and again that God's Word is the truth and we can believe it. *"Sanctify them by the truth; your word is truth."* – Jn. 17:17. Thus if we keep our lives according to the Bible, we can be sure that the truth lives in us.

But the truth can hurt too. It is painful when the Spirit of truth confronts us with secret sin, or reveals to us our shortcomings. We may not want to face it, but if we accept the truth about ourselves, we can confess it and by doing so, the Spirit of truth, who is our guide to a life of righteousness, will bring us ever closer to God and His Holy fire in which all falseness will be burnt like straw. This is what Jesus means in Jn. 8:32 when He says, *"...you will know the truth and the truth will set you free".*

Living in truth is more complicated than merely *not* telling lies. Jn. 14:17 puts it in perspective: *"the Spirit of truth. The world cannot accept him because it neither sees him nor knows him. But you know him, for he lives with you and will be in you."* It is clear from this verse that living in truth means completely embracing it, leaving no room for exceptions. If you are in denial about any aspect of your life, you are not living in truth. If you pretend to be happily married, when your marriage is in fact on the edge of divorce, you are not living in truth. The sooner you face up to the problems in your marriage, the sooner you can seek help to sort them out. If you accept your friend's apology, but still remain angry with her, you are not walking in the truth. Until you acknowledge your true feelings of hurt, you'll never be able to forgive her and move past your anger. You can put on a brave face and fool everyone, but you cannot fool God's Spirit of truth. It will find you out on every falsehood and lie.

I thank God for His grace. Eph. 2:8: says that we are saved by grace, through faith. Without grace no one would be saved.

Grace is a difficult concept for modern man to grasp. We can't understand why an Almighty God would just forgive us our sins and accept us. It is proof of His love for an undeserving people. His grace saves us from eternal death, it forgives our sin when we confess it, carries us through tough times and helps us to accomplish the things God wants to do through us.

Often times I've wanted to *do* something, *anything* to change Aldo's condition and when I'm exhausted from all my fruitless effort, I find comfort in the Spirit of grace as Paul did when he wrote in 2 Cor. 12:9: *"My grace is sufficient for you, for my power is made perfect in weakness...."*

Sy sal ~~Gse~~ God se bruid wees soos ek, God sal sy bruid leer wat sy moet sê en haar voorberei.

Wys soos weste suide noorde en ooste sy wil aan mense. Sy wil is sy bruid moet gereed wees. Sy moet sy bruid sê, sy maak haar ek gaan se sy gaan self die keuse moet maak om alles neer

WEDNESDAY, FEBRUARY 21, 2007

SHE WILL BE GOD'S BRIDE, LIKE ME. GOD WILL TEACH HIS BRIDE WHAT SHE HAS TO SAY AND HE WILL PREPARE HER FOR HIS RETURN. SHE WILL COME FROM THE WEST, THE SOUTH, THE NORTH AND THE EAST. IT IS HIS WILL THAT HIS BRIDE WILL BE READY WHEN HE RETURNS. WARN THE BRIDE, MOM. SHE HAS TO MAKE THE CHOICE HERSELF.

> 2 COR. 3:6: HE HAS MADE US COMPETENT AS MINISTERS OF A NEW COVENANT – NOT OF THE LETTER BUT OF THE SPIRIT; FOR THE LETTER KILLS, BUT THE SPIRIT GIVES LIFE.

To me this is the most important characteristic of the Holy Spirit; the covenant life in Christ. If it hadn't been for Jesus and His atonement on the cross, I would have no hope in this life or the next. The Spirit of the Covenant constantly reminds me of this and thus confirms and renews my relationship with God. His blood cleansed me from all my sin and inequity.

Whenever we share in the sacred sacrament of communion, we are renewing our covenant with God. The true meaning of the bread and the wine as His body and His blood is too often lost on us. When we eat the bread, as a symbol of the body of Christ, it feeds us and when we drink the wine (or juice) as the symbol of His blood, it quenches our thirst. For Jesus says in Jn 6: 55, 56: *"For my flesh is real food and my blood is real drink. Whoever eats my flesh and drinks my blood remains in me and I in him."*

This is my blood covenant with God: because Jesus took my sin upon Him I may escape punishment and receive life in abundance instead.

Every time when I eat the bread, I choose to die to myself; to give up control of my life, and every time I drink the wine, I choose to live a new life in Christ. The Spirit of Covenant reminds me that He has already paid the highest price for me so that I can have life eternal.

The table of communion is also the place where I search my heart to see if I'm still in rightstanding with God. It is the place where I confess my sin, obtain forgiveness and healing. In short, communion restores me in God's sight as I'm again covered by the blood of the Lamb.

But living in a covenant relationship doesn't only pertain to communion or what will happen to me after I die. It also determines how I conduct myself on Earth during the time I have left. If you are truly living a covenant-bound life, you cannot separate any aspect of your life from your covenant with God. It is impossible to accept or pay a bribe in business if you're living in covenant with God. Likewise you cannot be unfaithful in your marriage, and claim to live in covenant with God!

This is serious stuff! Look at what God says in Heb. 10: 29-31 about those who disregards the covenant: *"How much more severely do you think a man deserves to be punished who has trampled the Son of God underfoot, who has treated as an unholy thing the blood of the covenant that has sanctified him, and who has insulted the Spirit of grace? For we know him who said 'It is mine to avenge; I will repay' and again, 'The Lord will judge his people.' It is a dreadful thing to fall into the hands of the living God."*

1 April 2007

I love You, Jesus. You told me that we have to write a book, and we were obedient. God's blood and His Word will set you free. God wants you to have faith in Him. Don't put your trust in worldly wonders and things. God will blow His breath into this book and as you read it, you will feel His Spirit loving you; showing you the way. I love You, God. I love You, Holy Spirit.

Weet jy dat saam sal ons
wees in die hemel daar
gaan ons nooit weer
siek wees nie. Almal is
gesond en God sit op
Sy troon en Sy Seun
sit langs Hom.
Hy wil Sy bruid kom
haal maar sy is nie
gereed nie. Sy moet
haar sondes weerlê want
God se bruid is heilig
Mamma moet vir die
mense sê ons is die
Laudisia gemeente. God sal
Sy oordeel laat kom oor
die mense wat Hom nie
aanneem nie.

FRIDAY, FEBRUARY 23, 2007

DO YOU KNOW WE'LL BE TOGETHER IN HEAVEN, MOMMY? WE WON'T EVER BE SICK IN HEAVEN! THERE, GOD IS ON HIS THRONE AND HIS SON SITS NEXT TO HIM. HE WANTS TO COME AND FETCH HIS BRIDE, BUT SHE ISN'T READY YET. SHE HAS TO STOP SINNING BECAUSE GOD'S BRIDE IS HOLY. MOMMY, YOU HAVE TO TELL PEOPLE THAT WE ARE THE LAODICEA CHURCH. GOD'S JUDGEMENT WILL BE ON THOSE WHO DO NOT ACCEPT HIM.

> REV. 3:15,16: BUT I KNOW YOUR DEEDS, THAT YOU ARE NEITHER COLD NOR HOT. I WHISH YOU WERE EITHER ONE OR THE OTHER!
> SO, BECAUSE YOU ARE LUKEWARM – NEITHER HOT NOR COLD – I AM ABOUT TO SPIT YOU OUT OF MY MOUTH.

While we were having a cook-out one night, Aldo suddenly said, "Mommy, you have to tell everyone that we are the Laodicea church".

"What is he talking about?" asked Tinus.

"It is the last church mentioned in Revelations," I tried.

Aldo kept reciting the Scripture quoted above.

Since that night, Aldo often remarks that the world has to hear that we (the current Christian generation) are the Laodicea church and it is perhaps fitting that I should close this book with a few remarks to this lukewarm church.

If there is one person who truly knows you, it is God. He knows what you are thinking every moment of every day. He knows what you're striving for and why? He knows the reason why you're always trying to impress others. He sees you when there's no one else around. He observes your duplicitous manner: how you behave one way to your husband/wife and children at home, and then another when others are watching. You can't hide anything from God.

He knows your heart's secret desires. He also knows that you long to love Him more and that you're actually seeking to know Him more. He knows this, because He made you this way: To have a desire for Him. God sees right through us as if we were made of glass.

If I had to rephrase the Scripture in Rev. 3.15,16 quoted above in my own words, it would read something like this:

"Laodicea, you are a spineless, useless bunch! You want to serve God, but refuse to give up on mammon. You tithe when it is convenient, and attend church Sunday after Sunday so that others can see your piety. You are *so* religious and always eager to help a good cause, focusing on human rights and tolerance, instead of on Me. You are always looking for happiness in some worldly pleasure. And then you fool yourselves into thinking that you can bribe me with what little time you can spare for Me. You are self-centered and refuse to change."

I often hear people saying, "This is who I am. Either take it or leave it."

God's answer to this challenge is, "I'll spit you out of my mouth!"

God's message to all of us is the same as it is for the Laodicea church: Lukewarm water is good for nothing. At least cold water can quench a thirst, and boiling hot water can be used to heat cold substances, but lukewarm water is a waste. We have to be boiling hot for God. In fact we should be boiling over with His goodness and joy! Too often the church frowns on those who are boiling hot for Jesus – those Jesus-freaks who are completely sold out to Him.

Beware! There are no grey areas with God! He cannot stand hypocrisy! He calls those lukewarm Christians, whitewashed tombs and vipers (evil snakes). God hates sin and pride, but He despises our godless piety and criticism of those who are burning with the Holy Spirit for God.

The problem with the church in Laodicea was that although they confessed their faith, they were still in control of their own lives while Jesus had to remain on the outskirts of their existence. They were not moved by the Spirit. They would only act on the Word if they felt like it and they would only obey God if there was some marvelous sign in the heavens! They were *so* content with their own circumstances that they didn't want to walk on water!

If you're still in control of your life, and perhaps even of the lives of those around you, you'll definitely feel right at home in the Laodicea church. So many people have so-called "self-confidence". Listen to me: believing in yourself isn't the answer! You cannot do anything from your own power or resources, or haven't you had to face this fact yet? Don't believe in yourself! Believe in God. Have God-confidence! Only then will you realize that you "can do everything through Him who gives me strength" (Phil. 4:13).

If you're still part of this lukewarm, self-confident church, God's message in Rev 3: 17 and 18 is specifically for you. It reads: *"You say, 'I am rich; I have acquired wealth and do not need a thing.' But you do not realize that you are wretched, pitiful, poor blind and naked. I counsel you to buy from me gold refined in the fire, so you can become rich; and white clothes to wear, so you can cover your shameful nakedness; and salve to put on your eyes, so you can see."*

In this piece, God tells those lukewarm Christians exactly what to do to return to Him He tells them to buy a number of things from Him, i.e. fire-refined gold, white robes, and miracle salve.

The gold He will sell them will make them truly rich since it has been refined and all the impurities have been removed. When I hear people boasting in their possessions, I feel sorry for them, for earthly possessions can be stolen or destroyed. Only the indestructible gold of faith can never be destroyed. The fire will only make it purer. 1 Pet. 1:7 spells it out clearly: *"All kinds of trials have come so that your faith – of greater worth than gold....... May be proved genuine and may result in praise, glory and honor when Jesus Christ is revealed."*

Secondly, God tells them to buy white clothes to cover their nakedness. Once you realize the scope and nature of your sin, you will feel naked. And nothing can cover sin, but the blood of Jesus. You have to clothe yourself with Jesus' atonement in order to go into the wedding feast, or you too will be stranded at the gate wearing "clothes of mud".

And lastly, they have to buy salve from God for their eyes so that they may recover their sight. Before the accident I was spiritually blind. But now I see. The veil has been lifted and I can see the glory of God everywhere I look.

I want to draw your attention to a crucial part of this Scripture. God tells them to *buy* these things from Him. They have to pay for it, but not with money. The price for these things is laying down your life. Although salvation is free, it is not cheap, my friend. Seeing through spiritual eyes, wearing the Holy clothes of righteousness and possessing fire-refined faith will cost you the ultimate price: your life! Nothing less.

Let me tell you this today, I, Retha, thought that I had all my bases covered. I had everything under control including my salvation. I did everything a godly Christian should do down to routinely reading the Bible and praying. I even taught my children to pray. However, I never taught them to "wait on God," because I suppose I never thought He would talk back to us.

That all changed the day I stood in ICU while the machines were screeching and the meters indicated that the pressure on Aldo's brain was constantly increasing. Suddenly there was nothing I could do. I could just stand there: a witness to the out-of-control situation. It hit me then: The power of life and death is in God's hands alone. It is completely out of our hands. I would have loved to be able to do *something,* anything.

All I could do was fall to my knees and cry to God like I've never done before. When He knocked at the door of my heart, I opened it immediately, but I couldn't look up, because my nudity was overwhelming. He gave me a white robe and salve for my eyes and faith like gold. I'm ashamed that it took this tragedy before I was willing to lay down my life and open the door for Him.

The message to Laodicea and to every person who reads these words is very simple. Either you are with Me or against Me (Mt. 12:30). Something is either right or wrong; good or evil. There are no grey areas.

There is no in-between. In-between is to be lukewarm; "neither cold nor hot". Read 2 Cor. 6:14 carefully: *"... For what do righteousness and wickedness have in common? Or what fellowship can light have with darkness?*" You either choose God or you don't.

God's voice is still calling you today, right now. He is speaking to you when He says, *"Here I am! I stand at the door and knock. If anyone hears my voice and opens the door, I will come in and eat with him, and he with me"* –Rev. 3: 20. Won't you open the door to Him right now?

A COLOURFUL MOSAIC

This run and stumble journey that we're on has taught me one thing: It's all about love. We have to love Him wholeheartedly and love our neighbours like we love ourselves. Love is the only thing that matters.

There is only one way to show your passion for God and that is by overcoming your flesh every day. Get rid of your own stubborn will that wants to control everyone. Your will must die.

The last three years since the accident have taught me that God's love is the only way we can receive an abundant life. Nothing in the world can dull the pain and suffering we've had to endure. God alone sustains us. Growing in faith, I seek Him more and more. I hunger for God. When one is in the world too much, this hunger is lessened. If I spend too much time on worldly pursuits, I am like a child who spoils his appetite before the main course. I've had to learn to wait for the real meal. I've learnt to wait on God. My monologue prayers have changed. I now wait on God to hear what He wants to say. Having a love relationship with the living God, means you cannot commune in a "take-away-fast-food" way. When I wait on God, revelations, power and anointing always follow.

My only anchor is God's Word. It's the Truth. And to serve Him is wisdom. Feed yourself with the Word.

The phrase "to be more like Christ" used to be empty to me. Now it is what I desire most of all. The more time I spend in His presence, the more I want to be like Him. I want to reflect Him. 2 Cor. 3:18 reiterates this, *"And we who with unveiled faces all reflect the Lord's glory, are being transformed into his likeness with ever-increasing glory, which comes from the Lord, who is the Spirit".*

I had to hand over all control to Him. I accept and confess that Aldo's future is in God's hands. I believe that He has only wonderful plans for us.

My Spirit caught alight as I drew closer to God, because *"our God is a consuming fire"* (Heb. 12:29).

People often ask me how Aldo hears God's voice. Aldo only gave me a Scripture quote when I too asked him

this question. "Read Numbers 12:6-8, Mommy," he said.

"... When a prophet of the Lord is among you, I reveal myself to him in visions; I speak to him in dreams. But this is not true of my servant Moses; he

is faithful in all my house. With him I speak face to face, clearly and not in riddles, he sees the form of the Lord. Why then were you not afraid to speak against my servant Moses?" In this Scripture, Moses' sister, Miriam, was rebuked by the Lord for speaking out against Moses. She wanted to know why God spoke to Moses directly and not to the rest of them. Here God makes it clear that He chooses whom He speaks to and He has chosen to speak directly to Aldo. People are often skeptical about miracles like this, but perhaps this is another case of God using a simple child to teach those who think themselves wise.

The Holy Spirit reminded me that although the disciples had walked with Jesus and seen the miracles He performed, they still doubted Him. I guess some people choose to doubt and others choose to believe. It is my prayer that the Spirit of Truth will unlock that which might seem strange to those who read this book.

I'm thankful that I have the rare opportunity to experience the supernatural nature of God on a daily basis. Although He put us through the refiner's fire, He also wrapped us in the warmth of His love and protection. It would be impossible for us to live in this dark world without the fire that now burns inside us. His fire is a light that destroys the cold darkness of this world.

I urge you to seek God's fire with everything that's within you. He wants to give you His fire. Believe me, there's so much more for you than you ever dreamed of.

I praise God! He has taken the broken potsherds and created a beautiful and colorful mosaic.

I want to live in Your light, Lord.
You are the Love of my Life and my First Love.

Retha

Author and public speaker Retha McPherson is also the founder of Retha McPherson Ministries. She travels extensively around the world as an ambassador of the Kingdom of God to proclaim the Gospel of Jesus Christ.

The accident in 2004 set in motion a series of events that would change their lives forever. Retha scaled down on her professional occupation and stared growing in ministry until 2008 when Retha went into full-time ministry.

Retha McPherson Ministries is situated in Hartebeespoort, South Africa. To contact the ministry, please visit our website:

www.rethamcpherson.com
Tel: +27 (0) 82 610 5757
E-mail: officer@lantic.net
Postal Address:
Retha McPherson Ministries,
PO Box 793,
Hartebeespoort, 0216, South Africa

We would love to hear from you

Printed in Great Britain
by Amazon

25255368R00099